How to Diagnose and Correct Learning Difficulties in the Classroom

How to Diagnose and Correct Learning Difficulties in the Classroom

Joan M. Harwell

Parker Publishing Company, Inc.
West Nyack, New York

©1982 by

Parker Publishing Company, Inc.

West Nyack, New York

*All rights reserved. No part of this
book may be reproduced in any form
or by any means, without permission
in writing from the publisher.*

Library of Congress Cataloging in Publication Data

Harwell, Joan M.
    How to diagnose and correct learning difficulties
in the classroom.

    Includes index.
    1. Learning disabilities. 2. Remedial teaching.
I. Aitle.
LC4704.H38   371.9   81-16860
ISBN 0-13-405423-7   AACR2

Printed in the United States of America

The Practical Help This Book Offers

Several years ago, a wise colleague remarked that she "enjoyed teaching children with learning difficulties." As she succinctly put it, "Most kids will learn in spite of you, but these children only learn because of you." Since then, hundreds of children with learning difficulties have done "time" in my room. They have shown an average gain of 1.5 years growth for each .9 years of instruction in reading and 1.6 years growth for each .9 years instruction in math. These results are remarkable when compared with the prior years' growth shown by these youngsters when a gain of .3 years growth per .9 years instruction was typical. You, too, can get the higher gain by applying the techniques outlined in this book.

Illustrative of the results you can get is the case of a boy called "Mousie." He was in my seventh grade EH class (a California term meaning educationally-handicapped). One day, I asked him why everyone called him "Mousie," but before he could answer, two other boys told me it was because he was so small and quiet. "Mousie" later related that he rather liked the name and said he had acquired it in kindergarten. He then explained he had "flunked kindergarten because I kept running into the teacher with the tricycle." *At seventh grade Mousie was virtually a nonreader*—he confused *b* for *d*, *p* for *q*, *no* for *on*, *saw* for *was*; he couldn't tell an *e* as in *egg* from an *i* as in *it*; and his handwriting wriggled and wobbled all over the page. But Mousie wanted to learn! He listened and tried and *by the end of that school year Mousie was reading in second-grade readers.* Unknown to me, Mousie's father was fairly prominent in the area and my teaching reputation was made in that community.

By using these activities and suggestions, your teaching will become more effective. You will see greater results in the child's progress. In a short while the child's parents will note also that the child is happier, is more motivated, and has learned new skills.

Use of these activities will save you lesson-planning time, freeing you to pursue other projects.

If you must complete an Individual Educational Plan for any child in your room, the suggestions in this book can be of tremendous help in completing that evaluation.

Finally, if your teacher-training did not include classes in remedial instruction or classes on working with learning-handicapped children, this book will upgrade your skills by giving you a background in that area. You will feel confident with these children because, as you remediate, you will know exactly what you're doing and why you're doing it.

The purpose of this book, therefore, is to provide you with daily help in meeting the individual academic, social, and emotional needs of the children who have learning difficulties. *Many of the activities are suitable for all students in your classroom.*

Section 1 of this book addresses assessment procedures, learning styles, grouping for instruction, record-keeping, handling discipline problems, and grade-by-grade list of competencies to be developed.

Section 2 presents a brief statement of a particular learning problem with specific remediation suggestions. The case studies given in this section will assist you in having a "feel" for the child and give you some idea of the results that may be achieved. Included are 77 activities to aid in the development of language and conceptual thinking and a chapter on children who are hyperactive, hypoactive, or epileptic.

Section 3 pertains to specific skill development in subject areas of reading, math, and art. Chapter 10 has plans for 43 days of remedial reading and also 22 sample paragraphs. There are instructions for teaching 18 skills in remedial arithmetic. Art activities to improve visual perception and motor control include 31 projects in 15 media.

If the "back to basics" movement, competency legislation, and Public Law 94-142 (the Education of All Handicapped Children Act of 1975) have caused you stress, this book will be an invaluable aid to you.

Joan M. Harwell

Contents

The Practical Help This Book Offers 5

Section 1   DIAGNOSIS AND TEACHER PLANNING

1. Diagnosing Learning Disabilities in Children 13

    Making a Preliminary Class Study   13
    How to Do a Preliminary Screening for Children with
        Learning Problems   15
    How to Work with Parents   17
    Make a Proper Referral for Physical Examination   20
    How to Do an Academic Assessment   21
    Obtain an Assessment of Intellectual Capacity   22
    Do an Assessment of Preferred Learning Style   22
    Developing the Individual Education Plan (IEP)   28

**2. Managing Your Classroom for Greater Output Without
Increased Effort** 30

    Establish a Teacher-Pupil Working Relationship   30
    Develop an Effective Lesson Plan   33
    Establish a Workable, Effective Record-Keeping
        System   35
    Utilize Parent Volunteers and Student Tutors   36
    Have an Effective Discipline System   38
    Principles of Discipline   40

**3. How to Use a Grade-by-Grade List of Competencies
to Meet Individual Needs** 44

    Lists for Each Grade from Entry Level in Grade 1 Through
        Grade 6

Section 2 SPECIFIC LEARNING DEFICITS WITH SUGGESTIONS FOR REMEDIATION

4. Overview: Recognizing and Identifying Specific Learning Deficits 63

Importance of Body Awareness and Motor Control   63
Empathy   64
Feedback   65
Evaluation by the Teacher   65
Individualizing Instruction   66

5. How to Help Children Who Demonstrate Visual Perceptual Deficits 68

Visual Discrimination Deficits   69
Activities for Remediation of *B, D* Confusion   72
Remediation Activities for *P, Q*   73
Remediation of Inversions   74
Remediation of Letter Confusion   74
Remediation of Sequencing Problems   75
Teach Children to Look for Punctuation   76
Visual Figure-Ground Deficits   76
Activities for Visual Figure-Ground Deficits   78
Visual Constancy Problems   80
Visual Memory Deficits   83
Visual Association and Visual Closure Deficits   85

6. How to Help Children Who Demonstrate Auditory Perceptual Deficits 89

Auditory Discrimination Problems   91
Auditory Distractibility or Auditory Figure-Ground
    Problems   96
Auditory Memory Deficits   98
Activities for Increasing Auditory Memory   100
Auditory Association and Auditory Closure Problems   101

7. Helping Children Who Demonstrate Deficits in Body Awareness and Motion Control 106

Contents

How to Locate Children Who Need Specific Motor
Skills   107
A Program of Gross Motor Skills for All Children   107
Developing a Program for Body Awareness   112
A Program for Fine Motor Skills   117

**8. How to Help Children Who Demonstrate Problems in
Language Development and Conceptual Thinking 124**

Recognizing a Child with Problems with Language and
Conceptual Thinking   124
Class Discussion for Language Development   125
77 Activities for Perception, Conceptual Thinking, and
Language Development   127

**9. How to Help Children Who Demonstrate Problems in
Attention or Behavior 143**

Children Who Are Hyperactive, Hypoactive or
Epileptic   143
Children with Difficulties in Emotional Adjustment   147

Section 3   SKILLS DEVELOPMENT
IN GIVEN SUBJECT AREAS

10. How to Teach Remedial Reading 151

Visual Supports for Teaching Reading   151
Day-by-Day Activities for 43 Days   155
General Principles for Teaching Reading   176
Neurological Impress to Teach Remedial Reading   177
22 Sample Paragraphs for Neurological Impress
Sessions   179

11. How to Teach Remedial Arithmetic 184

Teaching 18 Arithmetic Skills Step-by-Step   185

**12. Improving Visual Perception and Motor Control with
No-Fail Art Activities 195**

31 Art Projects in 15 Media   196

A Few Words in Closing 212

Glossary of Terms... 213

Index 217

Section 1

DIAGNOSIS AND TEACHER PLANNING

1

Diagnosing Learning Disabilities in Children

This chapter will help you
- Locate the children in your room who need more individual attention.
- Assess these children for their individual strengths and areas needing improvement.

MAKING A PRELIMINARY CLASS STUDY

In a given classroom of thirty children, the teacher can ordinarily name at least four to six youngsters whose progress is a matter of concern. While experts continue to argue over "What is a learning disability?", we, as teachers, can easily spot children who are "out of step" with their grade level expectancy either socially, academically, or both. The degree of the problem ranges from mild to severe. The child's problems usually fall in *one or more* of these areas:

1. Perceptual problems.
2. Motor problems.
3. Attention problems.
4. Directionality-spatial relationship problems.
5. Memory deficit problems.
6. Language development deficits.
7. Conceptual thinking deficits.
8. Behavior problems.

There is no single child who is typical of all other learning-disabled children. Each child must be viewed in terms of his own strengths and weaknesses and a plan developed to meet that child's needs. Therefore, a careful assessment and written goals should be established as early as possible for each problem learner.

While each child with a learning problem must be considered unique, many of these children share some of the following common experiences. They may have experienced

1. *Repeated failure and motivational problems.* While all children fail sometime, the children we are talking about usually know they fail more often than other children. This realization frequently results in low self esteem and an "I don't like school" or "Why try?" attitude. Assignments are not done or are very poorly and haphazardly done.

2. *Frequent absence pattern.* Many children with learning problems have a history of multiple illnesses, such as ear infections and visual deficits. If the child has been in school for several years, frequent absences are often seen.

3. *Environmental upsets.* Children with learning problems often come from impoverished homes where communication between parent and child is typified by remarks such as "Go outside and play" or "Shut up." In early childhood, these parents usually confined the youngsters to a crib or playpen for most of the waking hours, thus limiting the child's opportunity to explore and discover. A few children with learning difficulties are reacting to a stress-laden environmental situation that saps their energy. Examples would be the illness and death of a parent or the divorce of parents following years of family turmoil.

Again we realize each child must be individually assessed before an educational plan is developed. If motivational factors and repeated failure are a part of the picture, we must insure that each assignment is fully completed as well as successfully completed. (Success does not imply 100% mastery, but it does imply that the child feels he did something worthwhile.) If physical abnormality is present, we must compensate for it. For instance, if a child has a hearing deficit, see he sits near the board, and make certain he hears instruction. Stand near him so he can hear better and watch your lips. Repeat or write instructions for him. Never show irritation should the child ask for your help. If environmental deprivation is obvious, provide the child with a rich language development program so he sees, feels, tastes, hears and learns words. Thus he can talk about all kinds of things. To

Diagnosing Learning Disabilities

the child, an orange is not just a "thing to eat" but can be described by the child in terms of shape, color, size, taste, and feel. Finally, if a child's learning problem stems from a situational crisis such as critical illness of a parent or divorce, genuine kindness and concern by the teacher are essential if the child is to function despite the situation.

At this point, you are probably beginning to put names with some of the problem areas cited. That's good ... it is the first step in utilizing this book.

HOW TO DO A PRELIMINARY SCREENING FOR CHILDREN WITH LEARNING PROBLEMS

Now take a paper, Write down the names of the children in your class who

a. Never finish an assignment or activity, or
b. Turn in work of significantly inferior quality when it is compared to the class average.

Now go back and in writing begin to pinpoint contributing failure factors such as noting which ones

1. Misbehave habitually—especially children who are constantly talking or out of their seats, pestering others.
2. Show records of frequent absences or tardiness.
3. Cannot give the names of common objects such as naming an orange or scissors and/or cannot tell you the function of common objects such as a toaster/clock/ruler/thermometer.
4. Show signs of extreme anxiety such as withdrawal (no friends in the class) or incontinence (urinating/defecating while in class) or crying daily.

You have now established a list of children who will need further evaluation by you and other members of the teaching team and who also need specific educational intervention to help them achieve.

Over the next two weeks jot down specific behavioral observations. Behaviors which are counter-productive to academic progress should be charted. Observe the child on three consecutive days for a five-minute period each morning and each afternoon. As you make these observations be certain the child does not know he is being watched. Why is this observation important? Often you can discover a specific behavior which explains why the child's work is not completed or is poorly completed. For example, one 8 year old girl I observed for a total of 30 minutes showed the following record:

Oct 2, A.M. (5 minutes)

Gave child a page of 20 easy addition facts which she "knew" (had demonstrated to me) how to do.

Behaviors displayed
Looking around.
Broke pencil,
went to sharpener.
Talking.

At the end of 5 minutes, she had no problems completed.

Oct 2, P.M. (5 minutes)

Art task—to copy simple animal step by step.

Looking out window—
out of seat.
Talking.

At the end of 5 minutes, she had completed step A (making a body). Most students were on step C, that is to say they had the body, head and legs drawn.

Oct 3, A.M. (5 minutes)

Drill sheet basic add facts.

Looking around.
Moved to another desk.

NO answers completed.

Oct 3, P.M. (5 minutes)

History lesson involving class discussion and teacher orally questioning various students re: material

Child yelled out asking to be called upon. When asked to answer, she said "Please repeat the question." The question was repeated, she responded "Oh, I don't know that" and began to look out the window.

Oct 4, A.M. (5 minutes)

Reading group. Student was one of 6 children working with classroom aide.

Lost place. Looking around. Talking to a child who was not in group. Kicking a child in the group under the table.

Oct 4, P.M. (5 minutes)

Children were told to meet teacher at the baseball diamond.

This child went to play tether ball, had to be called to group.

As a result of the above observation notes, I began some educational intervention:

Diagnosing Learning Disabilities

1. A conference was held with the girls' parents where I suggested strongly the child be seen by a pediatric neurologist. I sent a copy of my notes with the parents to the doctor. Ritalin medication was prescribed. Ritalin is a drug that usually increases the attention-span.[1]

2. The child was assigned a carrel in the quietest corner of the room with the fewest visual and auditory stimuli. There she was to do seat work.

3. Seat work was cut into smaller segments. The 20 problem math sheet was divided in 2 parts of 10 problems each. A reward of 10 peanuts was given at the end of each segment accurately completed.

4. The girl was re-assigned to a slightly lower reading group and the aide made a point to ask the child to read at least a few pages daily. This was very satisfying to the child because it enhanced her feelings of being important and able to accomplish.

Having made a chart of behaviors, share your findings and concerns with your principal prior to having a conference with the childs' parents. The principal, in turn, may wish to add observations he or she has made or he may wish to observe the child himself. Then you, jointly, are ready to discuss the matter with the child's parents.

HOW TO WORK WITH PARENTS

The goal of the parent-teacher conference is to establish a cooperative working relationship with the parents. In setting an appointment time and place, the parents' wishes must be considered. Often parents feel more comfortable if the principal and teacher come to the home. A home visit, however, should be a "scheduled" visit rather than an unannounced visit. Regardless of where this meeting is held, allow ample time. Neither principal nor teacher should be pressed to terminate the interview because of other commitments. The reason for this is simple. Most parents are quite upset when they learn their child is having school problems. Often they feel guilty—

---

[1] Ritalin, the preferred drug for hyperactivity, has the effect of increasing attention-span, alleviating some visual-perceptual confusion, decreasing impulsivity, and calming the child. The child normally takes two doses a day—the first about 45 minutes before breakfast, the second about 45 minutes before lunch. The teacher should observe and report to the doctor whether the medication is accomplishing the desired effect. If not, the doctor may need to change the dosage or switch to a new medication. Ritalin is contraindicated if it causes insomnia, loss of appetite, headache, stomach ache, depression, irritability or skin rash.

feeling these problems are somehow their fault. To establish a good working relationship, they need time to express and discuss these feelings. The following method is suggested in scheduling the initial parent-teacher contact.

The principal should send a letter to the parents. It should say:

> Your child's teacher, __(name of teacher)__, is concerned about __(child's name)__ because he/she is not making the kind of progress expected in____grade. We would like to have an opportunity to discuss the matter with you. A conference may be held either at school or in your home. Please phone at your earliest convenience so we may agree on a time and place for this conference.

At the time of the parent conference, ask the parents to have the child evaluated physically, academically and behaviorally, plus obtain an accurate measurement of the child's intellectual capacities. This evaluation may be arranged for privately by the parents or they may request that such testing be done by the school.

It is not uncommon for parents to want to deny the problem rather than face it. One thing the principal and teacher must guard against in the face of parent resistance is the tendency to be "too pushy" or "too wishy-washy." I remember sitting in on a conference once where the teacher had told me the child was "driving her crazy" but when the child's mother dissolved in tears that teacher said, "Oh he's a good child basically, and I'm sure we can work through these little problems he's having." The parent was then confused by why we were asking for a complete educational and medical evaluation. A better teacher response would have been "I'm sorry to have to give you such painful news, but together we'll try to help your son this year."

If parents are upset, it may take several conferences before they are able to accept the situation. Parents who feel frustrated may at first refuse the evaluation process but a while later accept it. Should parents not wish to have a child evaluated, that is their right. However, their objections should be carefully documented in writing.

Diagnosing Learning Disabilities

This documentation may later protect you and the district from a lawsuit.

Another possible pitfall for parents and teachers is the tendency to want to locate a "reason" for the childs' problems. The goal of diagnosis is not to establish causes but rather to assess the child's strengths and weaknesses so we can develop a remediation plan which will teach the child to do the tasks the world requires of him. However, if parents should ask questions about causation, educators need to be aware of several:

1. *Heredity*—research shows there is a tendency for learning problems to run in families.

2. *Trauma*—sometimes the cause of a learning problem can be traced to: (a) a traumatic pregnancy or delivery, (b) a head injury, or (c) a disease which caused a prolonged high fever.

3. *Developmental Lag*—some children just seem to mature more slowly than others. These children, with good teaching, often catch up with their classmates.

4. *Nutritional Factors*—recent research indicates diet may play a role in learning problems.[2]

As you share these possible causes with parents, they often come back with remarks such as, "His uncle Joe was the same way," or "Yes, she has always acted younger than her age."

It is also sometimes appropriate to offer parents reassurance. Some very famous people have had educational problems as children, for example, Woodrow Wilson had a very difficult time learning to read and Thomas Edison's mother was told by his teacher that "Tom is stupid." Parents should be encouraged to learn more about services for their children by contacting the following organizations:

> The Orton Society
> 8415 Bellona Lane, Suite 113
> Towson, Maryland 21204
>
> Closer Look
> Box 1492
> Washington, D.C. 20036

---

[2]Feingold, Ben F. *Why Your Child Is Hyperactive* New York, NY: Random House, 1974.

The Association for Children
  with Learning Dissabilities
4156 Library Road
Pittsburgh, Pennsylvania 15234

Once parents have agreed they wish to have their child assessed and the necessary written permissions have been obtained, a first step should be a complete physical examination.

HOW TO MAKE A PROPER REFERRAL FOR PHYSICAL EXAMINATION

Prior to making a referral to a pediatric neurologist, you will want to conduct an in-school evaluation of the child covering the following:

1. *Gross motor control*—Can he skip? Walk a line? Hop on one foot? Balance on a step stool or balance beam? Balance on one foot? Catch a ball? Toss a bean bag and hit a target? Crawl?

2. *Fine motor control*—Can he trace over lines, both wavy and straight? Reproduce a circle, triangle and diamond without confusion? Is his daily handwriting of poor quality? (include sample) Can he cut with scissors?

3. *Activity level*—Is the child constantly up and down? Is he easily distracted from tasks by noises or visual stimuli, for example, someone walking by? Does he over-react to funny episodes?

The school should send a letter of referral to the doctor via the parent, requesting an examination and a written report of fundings with notations of any implications that affect the childs educational program. Such a letter follows.

___(name of child)___ is being referred to you for a complete physical examination, to determine if there is any physical condition which may be affecting his school progress.

We have done an informal assessment of the following areas:

---

	yes	no	comments
Able to skip		x	
Able to walk a line	x		
Can hop on one foot (etc.)	x		does better on his right foot

We are attempting to design an educational program which will better meet this childs needs. Therefore, we would appreciate a written report from you including your findings, and suggestions for ways the school can help __(name of child)__ and if medicine is prescribed what is to be expected from it as well as the time it is to be given.

HOW TO DO AN ACADEMIC ASSESSMENT

Academic achievement can be tested by the classroom teacher, or a psychologist. Four simple-to-administer tests give a wealth of information about what a child knows and what he needs to learn:

1. The Woodcock Reading Test, Form A or B.
2. The Key Math Diagnostic Test.
3. The General Information Section of the Peabody Individual Achievement Test (PIAT).
4. The Wide-Range Achievement Test (WRAT).

The first three are available through American Guidance Service, Inc., Publisher's Building, Circle Pines, Minnesota 55014. They are self-explanatory and easy to give even if you have had no training in testing.

One point worth mentioning is this: It is helpful to record the student's incorrect responses on this test, as they often give a clue to what kinds of problems the child is having.

The WRAT can be ordered from Guidance Associates of Delaware, Inc., 1526 Gelpin Avenue, Wilmington, Delaware.

All of these tests are valid for K-8 students, but use Level 2 of the WRAT if the child is 12 years old or older. Each test can be administered in approximately 30 minutes. The student test forms should be retained as a part of the student's cumulative record.

HOW TO OBTAIN AN ASSESSMENT OF INTELLECTUAL CAPACITY

With written permission from the parent, the school psychologist may administer an individual test for measurement of intellectual capacity. The preferred test is The Wechsler Intelligence Scale for Children (WISC) Form R, 1974 which can be used for ages 5-15 years. This test renders subtest scores and valuable information regarding a variety of functions; some items test visual processes while others test auditory functions.

If the school psychologist administers the test, there should be a teacher-psychologist conference immediately following the testing so that information gained is shared. It is not uncommon to find a 20-30 point difference on the verbal and/or performance side of the test.

HOW TO DO AN ASSESSMENT OF PREFERRED LEARNING STYLE

In recent years there has been some research into learning styles. This research has implications especially in the teaching of the child with learning difficulties. It appears that some children tend to use one learning modality in preference to the others. This is particularly true of children having learning problems. Children who tend to learn more with their eyes are referred to as "visual learners" while children who primarily learn through their ears are termed "auditory learners." A third category is children who neither look nor listen but who are tinkerers; they learn by doing things with their hands. Research indicates that children with learning problems learn more quickly and thoroughly when instruction is given through their primary modality. These children, however, must also be encouraged to use other sensory organs to greater advantage and they can be taught to do so. By now you are probably wondering how you can determine a child's primary learning modality.

For the nonreader, this must be determined from the child's observable behaviors.

Primary Learning Modality

Observable behaviors	WISC scores	
Loves color, and movement. Art work shows many colors; much detail.	Higher on performance tasks.	**V I S U A L**
This person notices if you change bulletin board/you wear a new outfit.	Weaker on verbal subtests.	**L E A R N E R**
When reading, he comes to "funny," may call it "laugh"; sees "mother" says "mom," "bunny" is "rabbit."	Spelling sample—see page 25 this sourcebook.	
Loves noise, taps on desk; bouncing ball, frequently talks loudly and a lot.	Higher on verbal tasks	**A U D I T O R Y**
Speaking vocabulary usually fairly well developed.	Lower on performance tasks.	
Reads very laboriously, if reading aloud.	Spelling sample on page 26 this sourcebook.	**L E A R N E R**
Frequently whispers aloud when "reading silently" or doing math (because he has to hear it to learn it).		

Primary Learning Modality

Observable behaviors	WISC scores	
This child is in serious difficulty. He neither looks nor listens.	Weak on verbal.	**T** **A**
Usually is a nonreader.	Weak on performance.	**C** **T**
Easily frustrated. Cannot do because he has no skills to build on.	Spelling sample, see page 27 this sourcebook	**I** **E**
Pre-occupied with things—he may play with pencil, roll up paper wads. Likes to touch things, no respect for property of others, will touch and feel.		**L** **E** **A** **R** **N** **E** **R**
Puts things in his mouth.		
Touches other people. Rubs against you.		

For children with a reading grade level of 1.5 or better as determined by the Woodcock Reading Test, modality can be determined by a 20-word spelling test which you may administer to the individual child or group of children.

The technique below is an adaptation of a similar technique devised by Elena Boder, M.D., when Dr. Boder was working with dyslexic children.

First, administer a list of 10 words the child should know. Then administer a list of 10 words you know he doesn't know. It is important to tell the child you know he doesn't know them, but you'd like to see what kind of mistakes he makes. Encourage him to try each word even if he can only manage initial sounds. On the next few pages are samples of fifth grade student papers with an explanation of their analysis.

Suggested Word List

known	unknown
1. run	1. second
2. this	2. magazine
3. here	3. thimble
4. ride	4. poetry
5. yet	5. tired
6. eat	6. careful
7. park	7. develop
8. help	8. toast
9. stop	9. satisfy
10. duck	10. aggravate

Student A—Visual Learner

```
run          Sicut
this         magsing
he           thimble
ride         politree
yet          tirde
eat          craerfl
prck         bvelup
help         toce
stOp         stadis ie
Duck         aggav
```

Analysis: When you give a visually-oriented child a word to spell, frequently that child will look at the ceiling. The child is trying to remember what the word looks like. The visual learner almost always gets the first letter right and the word he writes is about the right length. Frequently the word written contains the correct letters but not necessarily in the right order (e.g., tirde for tired). Often the child remembers configuration—that is high letters, low letters:

|park| may come out |prck|

Student A's spelling test indicates that her primary learning modality is visual. Her observed classroom behaviors support this conclusion—for example, she rarely follows directions if they are given verbally, but follows easily if they are written on the board. The child has some deficits, however, in the use of her visual modality. She reverses *b*'s and *d*'s, and whole words such as *saw* for *was*. She is hyperactive and highly distractible (any movement will take her attention from an academic task). Finally, she will not look for directions on the board unless the teacher points them out individually to her.

Student B—Auditory Learner

```
run          Sakint
This         mugusin
hear         thimbul
ride         Poatree
gat          tierd
eat          carful
Park         Develap
help         tost
Stop         Satify
Duck         agravat
```

Diagnosing Learning Disabilities

Analysis: The auditory learner is easily identified. He tends to spell words phonetically (note his spelling of tost for toast, maguzen for magazine). Even if he has misspelled the word, a teacher knows immediately what he is trying to spell. His observed classroom behavior again supports our diagnosis. This child loves noise. He taps his pencil, slams his desk top, and even when reading "silently" is actually reading in a whisper to himself.

Student C—Tactile Learner

```
1. ron            11 sute
2. this           12 magz
3 he              13 thobe
4 rid             14 poith
5 gat             15 tibr
6 eat             16 Kot
7 prpK            17 d
8 hlp             18 tost
9 sapt            19 sat
10 д              20 arvgt
```

Analysis: This particular student is not performing as poorly as most tactile learners do, for he has had the advantage of receiving six months tutorial instruction via tactile techniques. Even so, you will note his performance on both known and unknown spelling words is markedly inferior to the visual learner (Student A) and the auditory learner (Student B). He hears less phonetic elements than Student A or B. Even though he can read *help, park* and *stop* without error, he cannot spell them accurately. In the classroom he neither looks nor listens. His hands and mind are constantly fidgeting with things he's brought to class—a toy car, marbles, whatever.

A typical tactile learner would show more distortions on initial sounds. Frequently these children are so frustrated they refuse to attempt to spell any words.

DEVELOPING THE INDIVIDUAL EDUCATION PLAN (IEP)

Having completed the behavioral, physical, academic, intellectual and learning style assessments, you now have the information needed to write an individual educational plan for the child. The following format and sample will serve as a guide for you.

Name:_____ Date:_____
Parent:_____
Address:_____ Phone No._____
Age:_____ Grade:_____
Present academic performance
   Reading-Woodcock Score_____
     specific deficit areas observed:
_____
_____

   Math-Key Math Diagnostic Score_____
     specific concepts needing instruction:
_____
_____
_____
_____

Psychomotor Skills needing instruction:
_____
_____

Behavioral Adaptation—areas of difficulty to be remediated:
_____
_____

Preferred Learning Style:_____

Diagnosing Learning Disabilities

Goal statement:

1. _____ New skill to be taught—Math _____

_____ technique, materials to be used: _____

2. _____ New skill to be taught—Reading _____

_____ techniques, materials: _____

3. _____ New skill to be taught—Psychomotor _____

4. _____ Behavioral change sought _____

_____ techniques to be used _____

_____ Comments of parent following conference regarding the IEP. _____

  The IEP will direct your teaching effort so you can achieve maximum results in minimal time. It should be reviewed often to assure you are on target.
  In this chapter was given a blueprint of how to find the children who need special help and assess their strengths and weaknesses—academically, behaviorally, physically and intellectually. You are now ready to begin teaching them more effectively.

2

Managing Your Classroom For Greater Output Without Increased Effort

This chapter
- Translates all the good educational theory you've had into sound educational practice.
- Examines ways to establish good teacher-pupil relationships and ways to develop effective lesson plans.
- Looks at record-keeping, discipline, grouping, and such issues as quantity vs. quality.
- Offers ideas on enlisting the aid of parent volunteers and student tutors.

HOW TO ESTABLISH A TEACHER-PUPIL WORKING RELATIONSHIP

As we have been told, the teacher-pupil relationship is critical to achieving maximum learning. It is important that, from the onset, your relationship to a child is positive—kind but firm—based on mutual respect. While this relationship should exist with all children, it must be pursued unfailingly with the learning-handicapped child. This child comes unglued when schedules are altered, seating is changed, teaching methods are unfamiliar, personnel changes are necessary (if you're lucky enough to have aides or parent volunteers). This child's need for *structure* is a paramount consideration. As you read this, you are reacting with realistic concern: "What do I do if circumstances force me to make changes?"

Managing Your Classroom for Greater Output

From experience I have found LD youngsters will accept change if you are considerate enough to enlist their cooperation. To illustrate, if the schedule must change, draw the LD children aside; explain to them why the change is necessary and outline to them what the new schedule will be. If seating must be changed, draw them aside, explain why, and if possible offer them a choice of new seating. If a choice is not possible, take time to tell the child you do care how he feels and that you are sorry you have to make him uncomfortable. Next ask him to try it and if after one week he is still unhappy to come—after class—to talk about it. My experience has been that nine times out of ten you will not hear from him, but if, occasionally, a child continues to complain after a week, listen to his reasons and, if possible, honor his requests.

When teaching methods are changed, be certain the child understands what he is to do before leaving him abandoned in his uncertainty. Uncertainty often translates into a failure experience (assignment is done incorrectly) or an invitation to poor classroom behavior. To make sure he clearly understands what to do, have the child repeat directions and demonstrate the process on 1-3 sample items. Writing short, readable directions helps the child remember. When personnel changes are made, give the LD child a few days to become accustomed to the new person being in the room before assigning this person specifically to work with this child.

Promises made to the LD child must be kept. To violate a promise upsets any child but it upsets the LD child terribly. His need for structure demands the promise be kept; if it isn't, you lose credibility in his eyes. It will take weeks or months to undo the damage done to your relationship.

Honesty is another essential of the teacher-pupil relationship. The LD child has suffered failure again and again. When he turns in an assignment poorly done, he knows it's bad. If you take the attitude, "Oh well, it's the best he can do," or "This is pretty good," when he knows he didn't understand it and it was lousy, you lose credibility. The child thinks either, "The teacher doesn't care if I learn," or "The teacher thinks I'm too dumb to learn," or "The teacher is a fool and I can just write any old thing down." If an assignment is poorly executed, say to the child, "__(name)__, I appreciate that you attempted this, but there are some parts we need to go over. I want you to understand it, so I will help you make the corrections." If it is not possible to do it right that moment, give him a time when you will.

This leads to another facet of a good pupil-teacher working relationship: specifically, the greatest educational value comes when *corrections and review closely follow the completion of an assignment*. If several days pass before papers are graded, you could better spend your time playing in the sand pile. My suggestion is that papers be graded immediately following their completion or, at the outside, later the same day. To accomplish this chore, you will need to (1) train the children to correct their own or (2) enlist a parent volunteer or a reliable, accurate child to help. As for the former suggestion, children as young as kindergarten can be taught to correct their own papers, but you must circulate and supervise them closely to be certain they are correcting honestly, attentively and accurately. When a mistake is made, it is wise for the teacher to help the child through the process and allow him to correct mistakes and then give some credit for a corrected paper.

Many times *children wish to share personal experiences* with the teacher. The teacher can not allow valuable instructional time to be frittered away by allowing all children to express themselves without restraint. A good technique is to say "___(name)___, I really would like to listen to you. Could you see me at recess or lunch so I can talk with you? I'm going to put your name on the board here to remind us we have an appointment." The loving, dedicated teacher relinquishes some free time to meet the students' social/emotional needs. When a new child comes into the class, an essential component in establishing a good relationship is making time to talk with that child. Ask him about his previous school experiences—questions such as, "Did you like your teacher?" "What do you like to do at home?" "Who do you live with?" All of these result in answers which give you clues about his attitude toward teachers, school and learning. At this time, share with him some things about yourself. For example, I often tell children, "I may seem mean at times, but I only get upset if you don't care and don't try. I really want all the kids to learn." Share with him some of the experiences your class has had before he came. Be a genuine, open, accessible person.

Whenever possible, *enlist another youngster in giving verbal commentation*. If one child says, "Hey, you read well!", support the child who extended the compliment by saying, "That was nice of you to say", (pat on arm) but add "And it's true. Good for you." (Pat child who was the receiver of the compliment).

Finally, *be warm*. Most children need touching. Touch often, but avoid touching if you see a child recoil. Recoiling indicates your relationship is not right (it may be that it's too early/this child comes from a nontouching family/the child is upset over past teacher experiences). Touching can be a pat on the back, shoulders or arm or a hand-squeeze. Boys tend to prefer "low-key" touching such as a pat on the shoulder or a quick embrace given without viewers. Young children generally like to be held briefly.

HOW TO DEVELOP AN EFFECTIVE LESSON PLAN

When I was in teacher training, we were required to write objectives for each lesson. I resented this laborious task in those days. After teaching several years, I found that by forcing myself to outline exactly what I wanted to achieve, I could prepare a lesson that was more productive in terms of the childrens' learning and one which moved along smoothly. I had fewer discipline problems. In planning a lesson, approach it from a diagnostic-prescriptive task-analytic stance.

Let's examine these terms.

Diagnostic/prescriptive teaching implies that each youngster be assessed prior to teaching. A simple teacher-made pre-test may be used or, in other cases, scores from a standardized achievement test may be utilized. For example, if you are working with a primary class and wish to teach them to recognize or make all the lower case alphabet, pre-test by asking them to write all the little letters of the alphabet. Analyze the results. You may have 8 children who don't know the alphabet; you may have 15 who know all the alphabet, but miss a letter here or there. You may have children who know most of the lower case letters but throw in an occasional upper case letter. *Teach* only those letters or elements each child requires. Don't bore a child re-doing that which he has already mastered. A second example might be in arithmetic (subtraction) with an intermediate grade class. Give a pre-test which covers basic subtract facts such as $9 - 5$, subtracting without borrowing, subtracting with borrowing. Analyze the results, then you can group children according to the skills each needs to master.

Task-analytic teaching implies that when you prepare a lesson, you will teach it step-by-step. For example, if you are teaching primary math, these are the steps:

1. The child must be able to count accurately to 10.
2. The child must be able to associate a number with its referrent, 7 = 7 beads, 7 blacks, 7 sticks; concrete counting experience is needed before moving to step 3.

3. The child must learn to add sums up to 10, using manipulatives or pictures at first.

   5 ● ● ● ● ●
   +4 ● ● ● ●

4. The child learns to subtract from 10 or a lesser number, using manipulatives or pictures.

   8 ● ● ● ● ● ● ● ●
   −4

5. The child adds and subtracts without the use of manipulatives/ or he draws his own picture.
6. The child commits to memory basic addition and subtraction facts 1 to 10.

As you write down your objectives, plan for

> FEEDBACK

If you only remembered one idea from reading this book, let it be a commitment to this principle—FEEDBACK.

Children vary in their ability to absorb and integrate knowledge. There are children who hear nothing that isn't said directly to them individually. At the mid-point we find children who hear and try to integrate but do so incorrectly. At the upper end are those children who absorb and integrate information accurately. You will want to ascertain that each child has absorbed and integrated accurately the knowledge you were trying to instill. You can check for feedback by asking questions, having children answer orally or in writing. Let us hope the feedback you get will not be as laughable as the following sample.[3]

Youngster Confuses Bowels and Vowels

SEATTLE (AP)—A fifth-grade pupil in the Seattle schools gave this description in a homework paper:

"The human body is composed of three parts: the Brainium, the Borax and the Abominable Cavity.

---

[3]This article appeared mysteriously, source unknown, on our faculty room bulletin board one day. It is typical of an LD child's confusion.

Managing Your Classroom for Greater Output

"The Branium contains the brain. The Borax contains the lungs, the liver and the living things.

"The Abominable Cavity contains the bowels, of which there are five: A, E, I, O and U."

Finally, in executing any lesson plan, it is a good idea to have a variety of materials on hand to insure there are enough materials for all children in the group. (Nothing is worse than running out of art supplies or dittoes). Provide a follow-up drill for all concepts taught at intervals commensurate with individual student need. For the LD child, a brief, weekly drill is generally essential to maintaining a previously mastered skill.

HOW TO ESTABLISH A WORKABLE, EFFECTIVE RECORD-KEEPING SYSTEM

Federal and state governments have thrust accountability and completion of certain forms upon us! The way I handle these is to do them immediately/keep them current day by day. This makes me look good to those who examine the records, helps me avoid panic as a deadline approaches, and insures that I do not forget important information. Often I have the child watch as I make a note on his record. I compliment his achievement. This builds his self-esteem and enhances his motivation.

However, long before the government imposed records on teachers, good teachers recognized the need for and kept records to help them focus on individualized teaching needs. So briefly let me present a few ideas:

Ms. Harwell's 2nd grade class									
Student's Name	knows alphabet	can write all lower case letters	can write all upper case letters	knows all consonant sounds	knows all short vowel sounds	knows and applies rules for long vowels	can alphabetize by 1st letter	alphabetize by 1st and 2nd letter
Blaine, Tom	✓	✓	✓	✓	✓aeio — uy	✓	—	
Castle, Jane	✓	✓	✓	—p,b f, v	— e, i	—	✓	—
etc.)								

✓ indicates mastery.
— indicates an area where instruction continues to be needed.

The pre and post test scores of children in a given subject:

Student's Name	1 Math level total (poss. 40)	Gain	2 Math level (poss. 50)	Gain	3 Math level (poss. 45)	Gain	etc.
Blaine, Tom	40 / 40	100% / 0	40 / 49	9	30 / 41	11	
Castle, Jane	23 / 35	12	31 / 32	1	29 / 31	absent fre-quently 2	
(etc.)							

Note in **red** if score is **100%**.
Note in **red** any factors influencing performance such as absence or illness or family trauma at test time.

In reading I require each student in primary grades to (1) read aloud in its entirety each story and (2) record words missed.

Student's Name	Story 1	Story 2	Story 3	Story 4
Blaine, Tom	they		Where	other
Castle, Jane	they	was, like, over	where	
Fisher, Genny	they	over		other, may

The _____ indicates story was read. The words missed are utilized to develop the class spelling list and are also incorporated into the dictation lessons I use to accompany the reading program.

Thus check lists, post-test score information, and the reading word list become instruments for planning future lessons and for meeting individualized instruction needs.

HOW TO UTILIZE PARENT VOLUNTEERS AND STUDENT TUTORS

To do an effective job of individualizing instruction, you must have help. Some teachers are fortunate enough to have paid aides. I have a paid aide but I also have 3 parent volunteers who come on a regular basis (2-3 mornings per week). Parents have a lot to give if

Managing Your Classroom for Greater Output

they are allowed to actively participate in the learning situation. At the beginning of each school year, I help the children plan a program or give a play to which parents are invited. Before the performance I assure that the children are letter-perfect and poised. Following the program, we have a relaxed party. During this get together, I circulate and meet parents. As we talk, I ask if they have small children at home or work. If they don't, I tell them I *need* help.

Many parents say, "I don't think I can help" and the reasons follow: "I didn't go past the fourth grade myself," or "I have a speech impediment so the children can't understand me," or "I like kids one at a time but a group scares me."

Each of these parents can be encouraged to help. The parent who only got to the fourth grade can help with maintaining class discipline by being your eyes when you're tied up. If the children are doing seatwork, this parent can help maintain a quiet environment by keeping an eye out for potential disturbance. For example, if a child leaves his work to pester another, the parent quietly says, "Is your work finished?" If the child says "No," the parent moves him away from the child he is about to bother and says, "Let's finish." If the child says "Yes," the parent moves the child into another activity. It is essential that a classroom have art work, puzzles, library books or interest centers where fast workers can go when assignments are complete.

The low-educational parent may be asked by a child for help. The parent can enlist a bright child to help the lagging child and supervise this liaison so the lagging child is taught by the bright one but not simply given answers or allowed to copy.

The parent with the speech problem or any similar disability can be encouraged to assist the teacher behind the scenes with typing, running dittoes, stapling, gathering supplies for art, etc.

The parent who is frightened by whole groups should not be asked to work with the whole group. He can listen to one child read or sit with a math dawdler, giving immediate feedback/help to one child. Later, this parent may feel comfortable and able to work with two, maybe three, children.

It is important to have parents present as group instruction is given so they see how you approach or teach a skill. They will emulate you.

When enlisting parent volunteers, at the beginning, you need to be specific. Don't say "Come anytime." Say, I need some help Monday morning from 9-10 to do (name it). If they say they can't make it Monday, suggest another day and a different need, but try to get a verbal commitment that they will come at such and such a time. They need to feel you are depending on them and you need to have definite ideas of how you'll use them. It is important, however, to have an alternative plan for the child if the parent fails to show.

It is also important to give parents *Feedback* on how they did at the end of each day: "Thanks for coming. If you hadn't been here, Pete and Joanne wouldn't have gotten to read." Have the children say thanks and ask the parent when he will come again. You may also add "I like the way you did [name a specific act] especially."

In most classes after a few weeks of school, you'll note some kids who like to help others. Utilize this "helping" urge and compliment the child for wanting to help. Be specific about how you want help given. Demonstrate by role-playing if need be. Keep a watchful eye to see if the helper follows through as you want it done.

HOW TO HAVE AN EFFECTIVE DISCIPLINE SYSTEM

In talking about discipline, we must always take into account why we need it—for the safety of all, to protect and enhance feelings of self-esteem.

The old adage "An ounce of prevention is worth a pound of cure" applies very well to our discussion of discipline. Careful lesson planning can preclude much misbehavior. Each child's learning situation must be success-oriented. Goals set for each child should be specific, and obtainable without undue frustration. Group the children in such a way as to meet individual instructional need. There are vast differences among children in terms of quantity, e.g., a fast child may do 100 problems in 25 minutes while a slow one only does 10. The classroom needs to provide enrichment activities for fast children as well as tutorial help for slow ones.

The length of instructional periods should not exceed 25 minutes unless: (1) opportunity has been made for some physical movement, and (2) the type of activity has been varied. You may wish to prove this in your own room. Give a long paper and pencil math assignment. The first 15 minutes goes well, then begins fidgeting, looking around, going to the pencil sharpener. The activity level increases steadily until 25-minute level. After that you will find more children who are not attending to task than children who are attending. If an assignment is 40 minutes long, plan a "break" after 20 minutes for a drink, to talk, etc. Tell the children you don't like to sit too long either.

Managing Your Classroom for Greater Output

The morning hours, nine to noon, are the best time for new instruction, particularly in math and reading. Afternoon activities may include

1. Art.
2. History
3. Social studies.
4. Music.
5. Science.
6. Physical education (an outstanding guide for physical fitness may be obtained by sending $2.00 to: President's Council on Physical Fitness, Washington, D.C. 20201)
7. Health.
8. Literature (Children love to be read to if the teacher is a dynamic reader and the story is interrupted for periodic questions with good answers receiving immediate positive rewards.)

A reward system adds excitement and interest to the school day. Rewards such as "good work certificates" or free time to use the class hand calculator (a good inexpensive item to have on hand, $15 at Sears) or doing a puzzle are stimulating to good students. Special self-directed art projects also are appealing to students.

Some children, especially children who have poor work habits and rarely finish an assignment, need a more tangible reward. They will work for stickers, balloons, pencils/erasers or edible rewards such as nuts, gum, crackers/cheese, raisins. The principle working behind rewards is simple. When behavior is positively rewarded, it tends to be repeated. It is, therefore, imperative that you only give a reward when the childs' behavior and work deserve it. If you reward half-done or poor quality work, you are conveying to the child that he can get by with mediocre work.

Unfortunately, teachers must also find ways to eliminate undesirable behaviors. To that end, we must use aversive techniques and apply them wisely. "Aversives" include things such as detentions, time out/ignoring, and negative feedback or reprimand.

Let us use the example of the frustrated child who may curse or throw his materials on the floor or say, "I won't do it." It is appropriate initially to try to avoid the situation that frustrates him. If the child has difficulty copying from the board or the book, the teacher should not expect the child to perform this task without an adult to guide his performance; for example, you can stand at the board erasing letters or words as he copies so he doesn't become lost or frustrated. While most children do this copying task with ease, the child with a visual figure-ground perceptual problem may become so frustrated that his emotional integrity dissolves and poor behavior is the result. Realizing his difficulty you may sometimes preclude the bad behavior by presenting him with the problems already copied. However, should the child curse and throw things, the bad behavior must be dealt with by aversive techniques.

The first aversive I use when a child says, "I won't do it" is *time-out*. The *time-out* aversive works this way: Tell the misbehaving child to take *time out* until he feels able to rejoin the group and meet his responsibilities. *Time out* may mean sitting at the back of the room alone, sitting in the office, or taking a walk to the restroom. If the child returns in 2-10 minutes in an acceptable mood frame, accept him back and make no mention of the episode. If the child is so upset that 10 minutes of *time out* does not settle him, he may need to go home for the balance of the day or to sit in the office until you can talk with him.

When the child returns, go to his side promptly and help him make an adjustment in the task so he can continue the task alone without frustration.

An additional part of good counseling technique is the process of modeling. Later the same day, by role playing, you can show the student a more acceptable way to handle his frustration; for example, to raise his hand and explain quietly to you or the aide that he cannot seem to copy the words. Have the child practice this technique and make a verbal agreement with you that he will try it when he again feels frustrated.

Ignoring is another type of aversive teachers may use. The child who is acting out or misbehaving because he wants attention should be ignored. For example, the child who shouts out "I know the answer" is not recognized or asked to give the answer until he learns to raise his hand and wait to be recognized. Be alert to call on him the first time he raises his hand and waits.

Social disapproval is an extremely powerful aversive. Bad notes home, spanking, and telling a child he has disappointed you are often effective, but should be used extremely rarely because of the devastating effects on the child's self image.

PRINCIPLES OF DISCIPLINE

Here are some principles you should find especially effective in disciplinary children:

Managing Your Classroom for Greater Output

1. *Do not use class time to deal with behavior problems*. Send the child to the office to sit or lie down until you have other children settled into their work.

2. *Do not discipline the child within hearing distance of his classmates*. Take some time to discuss what he did, tell him why he can't do it; have him repeat what you said so you know he heard you (frequently he is so upset he hears nothing); take time to model (role play) alternative approaches he can use should the circumstance occur again. (Example: Sam hit Bill for sitting in his desk. Let Sam tell you why he did it; you explain that hitting is not allowed at school as someone may be injured; have Sam repeat this rule. Then have Sam pretend to be Bill, you are Sam. You say, "May I please have my desk, now?" Reverse roles: he is Sam, you are Bill. Go through the modeling procedure but add, "If Bill doesn't move after you ask him nicely, what will you do?" Try to steer Sam to taking another seat and telling you about it at recess instead of stopping class right then to take care of it.)

3. *Do not ask the principal to handle your discipline*. Explain to the principal what you expect; that is, the upset child to lie down, but make it clear you prefer to handle the discipline yourself. Most principals will be cooperative and appreciative that you do not want to impose on them. I strongly believe children should be sent to the principal for praise—to show work well done. Try that sometime! You usually will have a happy child and a startled but pleased administrator.

4. *When some punishment is meted out, confine it to the day the poor behavior occurs*. Every day should be a new day for both teacher and child. It is awful to have a carry-over punishment to enforce when the child comes in happy. A ten-minute detention or a lost privilege is generally all the punishment needed. It satisfies the moral sense of justice to other class members.

5. *Discourage tattling unless it involves serious matters* such as stealing/bodily injury/destruction of property. Tattling frequently is an attention-getting technique used by the insecure child. The tattler becomes hated by his classmates—he is a "fink" and disliked by his teacher because he is constantly interrupting the educational process—he is "a pest." Teachers tacitly encourage tattling with subtle remarks and gestures such as: (a) "If someone bothers you, come tell me." (b) Patting/over-comforting the crying child. Children need help to learn when it's important to tell and when it's not. They should be encouraged to write their complaint down and hand it to the

teacher—understanding that the teacher may not get back to them till later.

When dealing with the chronic tattler, you can ignore his initial tattling as though you didn't even hear it. Later, at recess or lunch you find the tattler and ask questions such as, "Why do you think he called you that bad word?" or "Why do you think he hit you?" Ask the hitter or name caller to tell the child why he did it. Frequently, misunderstandings have occurred. Children need to learn that *all* behavior is meaningful; no one does something for no reason. Teachers must help children to see that the person on the opposite side of conflict has his reasons for doing the things he does.

6. *Help a child accept responsibility for his actions*. When caught misbehaving, most children try to shift the blame to another child, e.g., "I ran in the room because he was chasing me." You reply, "Oh, how did he make your leg muscles work?" When the child sees his responsibility, help him think of how he could have handled the situation in a more acceptable way. Do not let one child shift the blame to another. In the above example, finish dealing with the child who was running. Talk to the other child later about his part in creating the problem.

7. *Be a human being*. Let the child know you were a child once. "I remember doing the same thing you did once when I was a kid." Let the child know that while you do not care for the behavior, you do care and like him.

8. If a serious discipline situation exists, *keep anecdotal, written, dated records* as to what happened and what action you took. This kind of documentation in front of a child impresses him with the fact you do not want it to occur again. It also helps parents understand better if it becomes necessary to involve them in the discipline process.

9. *A give-and-take cooperative feeling must exist between teachers and students*. In general, learning-disabled students cannot take the authoritarian-dogmatic type personality—perhaps it intensifies their feelings of worthlessness. When accosted by this type of person, they often become mouthy, defiant or sullen. There are many ways a teacher may accomplish desired behavioral change. In illustration, whenever I encounter older children fighting, instead of sending them to the office, I begin to prance about with my fists clenched and saying ridiculous things like, "Let me at him." "I'm gonna get him. Yeah-Yeah." The effect of this absurd show is that both combatants and

spectators become amused and the fight is over. If there is an indication that it will resume, I invite both parties into my room—then in privacy, each combatant tells his side while I serve as mediator. When the matter is resolved, I send a report of the incident and its presumed resolution to the principal (communication lines must be clear).

SUMMARY

In this chapter are discussed five ways classroom management can be improved. Use of these techniques will increase your teaching effectiveness and will decrease some of the stress you may be feeling.

3

How to Use a Grade-by-Grade List of Competencies To Meet Individual Needs

To provide for a child's individual educational needs, I feel we need a checklist which will serve as both a guide to our teaching and as a record of the child's progress. Based on my years of experience, on the following pages you will find a suggested sequence of skills development that may be helpful to you.

> The skills shown under Grade 1 entry level may be accomplished, in part, in kindergarten, but must be considered priorities by the 6th month of Grade 1.

Grade 1   Reading/Writing/Language Development
—Entry Level (Goals to Be Accomplished by the End of the 6th Month of School)

The child will.
1. Recognize likenesses and differences in letters, geometric designs, words, pictures.
2. Write and name each letter of the alphabet in lower case letters, when presented in order or out of order.
3. Write and name each letter of the alphabet in upper case letters.
4. Relate a sound for each consonant letter of the alphabet (with

Grade-by-Grade List of Competencies

the exception of *y*), *c* will be called *k*, *g* will be called *g* as in *go*.

5. Relate short vowel sounds, *a* as in *apple*, *e* as in *egg*, *i* as in *it*, *o* as in *octopus*, *u* as in *up*.
6. Relate names to common objects; will not refer to objects as "that thing."
7. Relate simple experiences in an understandable manner.
8. Remember the main idea of a story read aloud to him and some supporting details in sequential order.
9. Enjoy listening to a story and participating in the discussion of it.
10. Talk in complete sentences.
11. Classify objects and relate them to his experience.
12. Follow oral instructions of one and two parts accurately.
13. Develop and demonstrate comprehension of

> up, down, big, around, small, little
> large, over, behind, under, near,
> before, after, beside, between, soft,
> hard, front, top, bottom, back

Grade 1   Psychomotor Skills—Entry Level

The child will

1. Write lower case alphabet legibly.
2. Write his full name (no missing letters).
3. Color within boundary lines most of the time (colors periphery first; interior second).
4. Locate a described subject, when shown a picture with multiple subjects.
5. Walk balance beam heel-to-toe (beam 3″ wide, 6″ off of the ground, 6 feet long).
6. Hop on one foot.
7. Be able to place finger on curvy line and follow its direction.
8. Toss bean bags approximating close a target at 5 feet distance.
9. Identify left, right.
10. Move spatially without undue clumsiness.
11. With scissors cut straight lines, and by turning paper cut wavy lines.
12. Paste neatly.
13. Match shapes, sizes, and colors accurately.

Grade 1   Mathematics Skills—Entry Level

The child will

1. Count numbers 1-10.
2. Tell which item is first, second, and third.
3. Relate a number to its appropriate picture set.
4. Discuss differences between sets in terms of more/less.
5. Name and recognize these shapes: circles, triangles, rectangles, squares.
6. Graduate items by size using terms such as small, smaller, large, larger.
7. Recognize common measuring devices by name and function, for example:
   ruler = a thing to tell how long something is.
   thermometer = a thing to tell how hot and cold it is.
   clock = a thing to tell what time it is.
   calendar = a thing to tell what day of the month it is.
8. Recognize and distinguish between a penny, nickel, dime, and give the value of each.
9. Add sums of less than 10.
10. Subtract sums less than 10.

Grade 1   Spelling Skills—Entry Level

The child will spell these words with 95% accuracy:

a	did	look	to
and	do	man	top
as	dog	me	tub
ask	fed	no	up
at	fun	not	us
bad	go	old	we
be	got	on	went
bed	had	one	will
big	has	pat	
but	hat	pit	
can	he	pot	
cat	I	put	
come	if	sat	
cold	in	see	
cut	is	sit	
dad	it	the	

Grade-by-Grade List of Competencies

Grade 1   Reading/Writing/Language Development (Goals to be Accomplished by the 9th Month of School)

The child will

1. Decode words of 3-4 letters (consonant-short vowel combinations).
2. Apply the rule that says an *e* on the end of a word makes the first vowel sound like its name.
3. Apply 2-vowel rule as in *rain*.
4. Enjoy/take part in simple plays.
5. Repeat letters in alphabetical order from memory.
6. Alphabetize a 5-word list by first letter.
7. Recognize special combinations *al, all, ar, ing, ow, ou, er, th, y* which says *i* on the end of words.

Grade 1   Psychomotor Skills (Goals to Be Pursued 7th-9th Month of School)

The child will

1. Continue repetition of established skills.
2. Trace accurately.

Grade 1   Mathematics Skills (Goals to Be Accomplished by End of Grade 1)

The child will

1. Count from 1-100.
2. Count first, second, third, etc., to tenth.
3. Understand the concept of nothing, 0, empty set.
4. Understand + sign means "put together."
5. Understand − sign means "take apart."
6. Understand = means "two sets are equal or represent the same number of objects."
7. Draw circle, square, triangle freehand.
8. Divide things in ½.
9. Name days of the week in order.

Grade 1   Spelling Skills (Goals to Be Pursued 7th-9th Month of School)

The child will spell entry level words of up to 5 letters with 90% accuracy:

about	five	into	open	star	wait
all	found	its	our	start	wall
after	four	jump	over	stop	walk
are	gave	just	play	sun	want
ate	get	keep	rain	talk	was
away	girl	let	ran	take	well
bad	goes	like	read	tell	were
ball	going	live	ride	that	what
best	good	lost	round	there	when
blue	green	lot	run	these	where
bring	help	mad	sad	they	why
boy	her	made	said	thing	with
by	here	make	same	this	woman
call	hid	may	say	those	work
came	hide	must	seven	three	yes
coat	him	my	sing	today	you
down	his	never	six	try	your
eat	hold	nine	sleep	two	
fast	home	now	small	under	
fall	house	of	smart	upon	
far	how	on	stab	us	
feet	I	one	stand	very	

The competencies outlined at Grade 1 constitute a monumental task for both teachers and students, but fortunately most school districts begin these tasks in kindergarten and continue them in first grade. The kindergarten and first grade teacher must (1) carefully plan what will be accomplished, (2) enlist sufficient parental support and help to accomplish the tasks and, (3) closely monitor each childs' progress utilizing checklists.

It is my strong recommendation that a child be retained in grade 1 if the child is significantly lagging behind the goals set. Many children need extra time to grow up physically and adjust to school routines and tasks.

Some children come to their initial school experience with well-developed vocabularies and alert senses (they show attention to visual/auditory/tactile details and are able to integrate academic learning into their already developed worldly senses). Other children are not so fortunate. Their vocabularies are limited; they are disorganized; they flit from activity to activity, absorbing only a small portion of the learning experience. These children desperately need additional educational intervention at this point in order to develop their perceptual abilities. They need a multitude of experiences designed to help them see, hear and feel in greater detail. They need time to talk with other children and adults (feedback) in order to relate new experiences to their environment. One year of first grade is not enough time for these children. I recommend that these children be allowed to repeat the grade with parents and district, providing increased opportunities for them including:

1. Special materials to increase visual, auditory and tactile stimulation;[4]
2. Closer adult supervision designed to allow the child greater verbal interaction and a more individualized approach to learning;
3. Special opportunities in the form of field-trips, audio-visual experiences (movies/filmstrips), learining centers all under close adult supervision.

Retention is Grade 1 need not be traumatizing to the child if we convey to parents and child alike that the child simply needs additional time to master basic skills. The child who gets a strong foundation in skills in Grade 1 (*masters* competencies outlined), and develops good work habits early, will usually progress through the balance of his school experience with minimal frustration, good achievement, and a positive attitude toward teachers and school.

Grade 2   Reading/Writing/Language Development

The child will

1. Recognize, and associate the correct sound with letter combination, i.e. *pl* is not *p* ... *l* ... , but *pl*; *sh, ch, oi/oy, spr, str, au/aw*.

---

[4]Some excellent programs are available:
Marianne Frostig's *Program for Development of Visual Perception*—a kit available form Follet Publishing Company containing worksheets for development of visual abilities;
Selma Herr's *Perceptual Communication Skills*, Program 1—available from Instructional Materials and Equipment (an auditory skills development program);
Jack Capon's *Perceptual Motor Lesson Plans* from Front Row Experience Company for development of motor skills.

2. Understand *y* has 3 possible sounds—*y* as in *yes, you*; *i* as in *my, type*; *e* as in *happy, dirty*.
3. Realize *y* and *w* are used both as consonants and vowels and can attack a word such as *snow* or *way*, and explain what the *w* or *y* is doing.
4. Understand use of plural form *s, es*.
5. Recognize suffixes *es, ed, ing*, and use correct tense in sentence development.
6. Write sentences independently, capitalizing the first word of each sentence, pronoun *I*, names of people, titles; and understand the function of punctuation !, ?, ., using them correctly in habitual fashion.
7. Develop and demonstrate an understanding of word families and rhyming e.g.:

and	ar	ight
band	bar	fight
hand	car	light
land	far	might
sand	jar	night
	par	right
	star	sight

8. Read aloud fluently, not haltingly.

Note: Teach child to read a full sentence silently before reading it aloud. Teach him to recognize the !/?/. as a stop sign—these marks represent the end of a complete thought.

9. Extract meaning from material read—main idea of paragraph; read and retell/write story highlights in proper sequence, sifting out nonessential elements.
10. Use context to unlock meaning/unknown words.
11. Distinguish between reality and fantasy.
12. Follow simple written directions of one or two steps.
13. Write independently complete sentences using correct punctuation, spacing.
14. Alphabetize word lists up to 10 words utilizing first and second letters.

Grade 2   Psychomotor Skills

The child will
1. Continue repetition of previously learned skills with increased refinement—tracing, cutting, pasting.
2. Develop better hand-to-eye coordination through bean bag or ball throwing/catching.

Grade-by-Grade List of Competencies

    3. Reproduce geometric designs or pictures when given step-by-step assistance.
    4. Skip.
    5. Jump rope.
    6. Develop arm muscles—bar pullups, push-ups.

Grade 2   Mathematics Skills

The child will
1. Count and write numbers to 999.
2. Count by 2's.
3. Count by 5's.
4. Count by 10's.
5. Understand place value—ones, tens, hundreds.
6. Add/subtract any number with up to 3 places without carrying and/or borrowing.
7. Add/subtract any number with up to 2 places with carrying and/or borrowing.
8. Measure inches/half inches accurately.
9. Recognize and use fractions—½, ⅓, ¼, ⅔, ¾.
10. Commit basic add/subtract facts to memory and drill these to the automatic recall level.
11. Use calendar—know sequence of days, months.
12. Measure using cup, pint, quart, gallon.
13. Count money—pennies, nickels, dimes, quarters—accurately.
14. Tell time by the hour and ½ hour.
15. Read accurately and work simple addition/subtraction story problems.

Grade 2   Spelling Skills

The child will spell with 80% accuracy words taken from the child's reading material. Dictation will be used to make this determination.

Grade 3   Reading/Writing/Language Development

The child will
1. Continue repetition of previously mastered words and read aloud fluently.
2. Recognize/decode compound words; words with prefixes *de, re, com, con, un, pre, pro,* and words with suffixes *ly, tion/sion, ment.*

3. Recognize and convert contractions to their literal meaning, e.g., *can't* is short for *cannot*.
4. Know rules for comma and utilize commas where appropriate, e.g., city from state, words in series.
5. Know and use possessive form *'s*.
6. Identify topic sentence in a paragraph.
7. Utilize connecting words in his writing; i.e., *so, but, when, then, next, finally.*
8. Recognize homonyms, e.g. *(sea/see)* and distinguish the meaning by spelling.
9. Develop language prowess through study of synonyms and antonyms.
10. Approach new longer words by habitually looking for syllables and known word parts—know and apply *vcv* rule, *vccv* rule.
11. Form his own sentences and paragraphs of at least 5 sentences.
12. Develop longer more descriptive sentences utilizing clauses telling where, when, why.
13. Write in sequence all lower case and upper case letters in cursive form.
14. Alphabetize utilizing first, second, third letters.
15. Understand and use dictionary to obtain meanings of unknown words.
16. Analyze reading words and give their phonetic spelling, e.g., *phone* is *f ō n*.
17. Use table of contents.
18. Write friendly letter in correct form.
19. Continue to extract meaning from stories; read some silently, some aloud.

Grade 3   Psychomotor Skills

The child will

1. Carefully examine and reproduce in intelligible drawings items seen.
2. Participate in jogging, arm exercise, hopping, tummy-development exercises and dodge ball with enjoyment and regard for fellow-participants.

Grade 3   Mathematics Skills

The child will

1. Count/write including numbers to 9999. Child can "guesstimate" how many beans are in various sized containers.
2. Understand place value—ones, tens, hundreds, thousands.
3. Understand and locate number patterns, e.g., 5, 10, 15, ___, 25, 35; 3, 6, 9, ___, 15, ___, 21; 102, 104, 106, ___, 110.
4. Pass with 90% accuracy a timed (10 minute) test of 100 basic add/subtract facts.
5. Add/subtract numbers involving up to 3 columns utilizing carrying/borrowing appropriately.
6. Understand and write number sentences:

    $3 + 4 = 7$
    $4 + 3 = 7$
    $7 - 3 = 4$
    $7 - 4 = 3$

    and realize that in adding and subtracting, the order does not change the answer.
7. Understand concept of multiplication, e.g., $2 \times 3 = 6$ is 2 groups of 3 things makes a total of 6 items. Demonstrates this knowledge through drawing accurate pictures such as

8. Understand the relationship of division to multiplication:

    $2 \times 3 = 6$
    $3 \times 2 = 6$
    $6 \div 2 = 3$
    $6 \div 3 = 2$

    and realize that in multiplication/division order does not change the answer.
9. Commit times tables 1-5 to memory at the automatic level.
10. Compare ½'s, ⅓'s, ¼'s and tell if they are bigger or smaller than one another.
11. Read and work accurately, simple story problems involving +, −, ×, ÷. Student will demonstrate correctness of operation by showing process in pictorial form.

12. Know how many inches are in a foot, how many feet are in a yard. Child can crudely "guesstimate" distance using his body to measure. *Note:* An inch being crudely the distance represented by one joint of the thumb.
    A foot being crudely represented by child's foot + 3 inch space.
    A yard being crudely represented as the distance from one's nose to fingertips with arm outstretched.
13. Tell time accurately.
14. Count money and make change up to $1.00 in fashion used by a store salesperson when giving change to a customer.

Grade 3   Spelling Skills

The child will spell with 80% accuracy, words from his reading book, as dictated to him.

Grade 4   Reading/Writing/Language Development

The child will

1. Read aloud fluently from reading series.
2. Tell and write summaries for stories read, selecting main ideas but leaving out trivia.
3. Adjust speed of reading according to purpose for reading.
4. Scan for information by using key words or phrases to locate information.
5. Give correct meaning for one word selected from a phrase or sentence by its function in that sentence.
6. Identify specific facts that add support to important ideas or add interest to the setting or understanding of characters' actions or personality.
7. Recognize and use words that indicate sequence; e.g., next, then, so, now, while, as.
8. Accurately predict what will happen next.
9. Compare two pieces of literature for likenesses and differences.
10. Recognize opinion versus fact.
11. Demonstrate improved quality of handwritten work in
    spacing.
    neatness.
    development of ideas by use of phrases.

Grade-by-Grade List of Competencies

12. Demonstrate vocabulary development weekly by using newly introduced words in his own sentences.
13. Participate in choral reading/dramatization by demonstrating ability to be appropriately expressive.
14. Appreciate and memorize 5 pieces of poetry.
15. Put words in alphabetical order.
16. Use guide words to locate word in dictionary.
17. Use index to locate information.
18. Use card catalogue to locate books in library.
19. Write short reports (1 page) that include a title, topic sentence, supporting details, correct punctuation and capitalization.
20. Identify nouns, verbs, and adjectives correctly.

Grade 4   Psychomotor Skills

At grade 4, the child should be involved in a regular physical fitness program such as the President's Physical Fitness Program, Washington, D.C. 20201, cost $2.00.

Grade 4   Mathematics Skills

The child will

1. Count, write, and understand place value to millionth place.
2. Pass timed (5 minute) test on 100 basic addition/subtraction facts with 100% accuracy.
3. Commit to memory times tables 6-10.
4. Add/subtract numbers with up to four places with or without carrying/borrowing.
5. Multiply a four place number by one place number.
6. Solve division problems involving a 1 place divisor and up to a 3 place quotient which may include a remainder.
7. Use arithmetic terms in relation to their function:

plus	minus	times	divisor
addend	minuend	factor	dividend
total	subtrahend	product	quotient
	difference		

8. Add/subtract numbers with decimals. In the case of money, child shows $.
9. Convert inches to feet, feet to yards, and vice versa.

10. Measure to nearest ¼ inch.
11. Identify parallel lines, figure perimeter, and understand terms such as radius, diameter and circumference of a circle.
12. Convert cups to pints, pints to quarts, quarts to gallon, and vice versa.
13. Know how many minutes in an hour, hours in a day, days in a week/month/year.
14. Solve story problems involving increasingly harder words and more than one process, e.g., Jim had 4 pieces of gum. He gave Pat 2 pieces. He bought 10 more pieces of gum. How many pieces does Jim have now?

Grade 4   Spelling Skills

The child will spell accurately 80% of his reading words as determined by dictation.

Grade 5   Reading/Writing/Language Development

The child will

1. Decode new words in his reading series using structural analysis skills.
2. Read fluently and comprehend central themes from his reading.
3. Recognize that punctuation can change meaning.
4. Continue to develop his knowledge of synonyms, antonyms, homophones, words with multiple meanings, and word classification.
5. Distinguish cause and effect relationships and predict what will happen next.
6. Perform tasks required by written directions (up to 3 directions involved).
7. Evaluate validity of reading material, making judgments from personal experience.
8. Develop and demonstrate the ability to translate a story into play form with consideration for character of players, setting.
9. Use encyclopedias, atlases, and almanacs to locate and obtain information, making notes.
10. Write twenty or more 2-3 page reports on a given subject, giving title, using and developing topic sentences. Child will give attention to paragraph development, including sentence structure, punctuation, capitalizing, spacing and legibility.

Grade-by-Grade List of Competencies

11. Give five oral reports of approximately 5 minutes length, utilizing appropriate visual support materials.
12. Use the following suffixes and prefixes correctly:

    | auto | dis | tion | ly |
    | un | re | tive | ment |

13. Continue to develop skill in using indexes, tables of content, and card catalogues.
14. Recognize subject/verb agreement and develop an understanding of verb tense—past/present/future.

Grade 5   Psychomotor Skills

The child will continue to participate in the President's Physical Fitness Program.

Grade 5   Mathematics Skills

The child will

1. Maintain knowledge of place value to millions place.
2. Drill basic multiplication and division facts to automatic level, e.g., completes a 100 item test in 5 minutes with 95% accuracy.
3. Multiply with up to 3 place factors, e.g., $\begin{array}{r}1320\\ \times\ 254\end{array}$
4. Understand relationship of multiplication and division, and can check division problems with or without remainders by multiplying.
5. Supply missing factors in adding/subtracting, multiplying/dividing when given the answer and one other part of the problem.
6. Compare fractions as to size $2/3:5/6$ and $1/2:3/4$. He will also add and subtract fractions and mixed numbers with like and unlike denominators.
7. Add, subtract and multiply accurately, numbers with decimals.
8. Measure accurately to $1/8''$.
9. Understand and demonstrate ability to convert ounces to pounds, pounds to tons.
10. Understand centimeters, meters, kilometers; grams, kilograms; liters.
11. Find an "average."

12. Measure and compute square feet, square yards.
13. Read and use graphs (bar/pie) and tallies.

Grade 5   Spelling Skills

The child will spell with 80% accuracy, words from his reading series in dictation practice.

Grade 6   Reading/Writing/Language Development

The child will

1. Continue to read and comprehend appropriate grade level of reading series.
2. Utilize dictionaries, glossaries to develop knowledge of word meaning.
3. Continue to demonstrate habitual use of capitalization, punctuation, and paragraph development in written reports of 8-10 page length.
4. Outline reports.
5. Diagram sentences in terms of subject, verb, phrases.
6. Expand vocabulary through regular weekly dictionary practice which results in utilizing new words in his own sentences.
7. Expand his knowledge and appreciation of poetry through memorization.
8. Participate in panel discussions/oral reports/simple debates.
9. Take written notes from oral reports of others, utilizing topics and supporting details.

Grade 6   Psychomotor Skills

The child will continue to participate in the President's Physical Fitness Program.

Grade 6   Mathematics Skills

The child will

1. Understand decimal place values of less than 1 to hundredths place.
2. Add/subtract any group of numbers with or without borrowing.
3. Multiply accurately up to 3 places with or without decimals.
4. Divide decimal numbers accurately with or without decimals.

Grade-by-Grade List of Competencies

5. Add/subtract/multiply/divide any fractional numbers accurately.
6. Demonstrate ability to utilize all 4 processes accurately in story problems.
7. Continue to utilize knowledge of measurement—linear, weight, time.
8. Handle all sums of money accurately; make change.

Grade 6   Spelling Skills

The child will continue to spell with 80% accuracy, words from his reading series as determined by bi-weekly dictation lessons.

In this chapter, I have outlined a guide to your teaching of skills. Transfer each skill into a checklist and record when a child achieves that skill. Insist on fluency and comprehension in reading. Be certain to provide for frequent opportunities to develop written and oral skills and, above all, utilize regular dictation practice to strengthen recall spelling of standard vocabulary. These dictation lessons, if properly developed, also strengthen the child's understanding of how words and phrases can be combined to achieve true communication.

By the time a child leaves the 6th grade, he should be equipped with the work habits and study skills necessary to be an independent worker at the junior high level. His use of written language should be well-developed because this will be his primary mode of giving feedback to his secondary school teachers. He needs to be able to read with comprehension and enjoyment, a variety of materials, relating the information garnered to his own experience and weighing it for its validity and relevance to his own experience. If we, as elementary teachers, achieve these goals, we launch a child onto a success-oriented educational pathway.

Section 2

**SPECIFIC LEARNING DEFICITS
WITH
SUGGESTIONS FOR REMEDIATION**

4

Overview: Recognizing and Identifying Specific Learning Deficits

IMPORTANCE OF BODY AWARENESS AND MOTOR CONTROL

It is hard in practice to separate remediation of visual perceptual problems from remediation of body awareness and motor control problems. The reason for this lies in feedback. An example is this: Let's say a child cannot identify a triangle. You would diagnose this disability as a problem of visual perception, but in your teaching you not only want him to be able to recognize and name a triangle but you will also teach him to reproduce a triangle free-hand (and this requires motor skills as well as visual perceptual skills). Therefore, in the coming chapter when I identify a visual perceptual problem, the activities for remediation usually will include motor activities as well as perceptual activities.

Under the chapter on Body Awareness and Motor Problems, I will suggest activities designed to increase a child's ability to follow directions, move without undue clumsiness, and develop greater control of certain muscle groups. These activities will not necessarily increase the child's ability to read or do math, but they are extremely important to increasing his ability to perform in daily nonacademic activities, and improving his self-concept. They will produce a stronger body which may, in turn, help the child in his eventual occupational pursuit.

EMPATHY

As you approach remediation you must have great empathy with the LD child. This empathetic understanding will allow you develop the patience required to be helpful to the child.

Children have a great need for warmth, affection, and praise. They earnestly want their teacher, their parents and their peers to like them. Learning-disabled children have these same needs, and when these needs are met by important people in the child's environment, the child is able to function with fewer behavioral problems. The typical learning-disabled child develops a poor self-image rather early in life because no matter how hard he tries, he winds up with someone fussing at him for something he has done wrong. All children have these experiences of being "chewed out," but they happen so frequently to the learning-disabled child (and praise for work well done is so rare) that he develops a rather negative attitude. He thinks, "I'm dumb," "Nobody likes me," or "Why try? Who cares?" The older the learning-disabled child gets before someone recognizes his basic problem and helps him deal with it, the harder it is to get through to him.

The child who is falling behind in his academic work acutely feels a sense of failure. This sense of failure is amplified if the teacher uses the designation, F, on a paper. This is a signal to the child and all his peers who are aware of the grade that he has failed and his work is worthless.

Children are sensitive to other signs of parental or teacher devaluation. One of the biggest put-downs occurs in the child's mind if the adult sighs. A sigh to a child means, "This child is hopeless." This may not be the teacher's/parent's feeling at all, but most children interpret a sigh this way. By the time the learning-disabled child reaches your classroom (even a primary classroom), the child may be evidencing the *failure syndrome* in words such as "I can't do this," or "I don't want to do this," or in actions such as simply not getting any work done.

If this syndrome is present, you need to understand the dynamics involved. The child feels he/she cannot do anything worthwhile so why try? To overcome this syndrome requires time, encouragement, love, and a concerted effort. This child needs daily success experiences in order to overcome his sense of inadequacy. He will probably also require the physical presence of an adult at his side to keep him

Specific Learning Deficits

working. As he proceeds, he may ask, "Is it right?" at intervals so frequent that it creates a feeling of annoyance in the adult, but he needs assurance at every step!

The teacher who expects all children to accomplish the same amount of work in the same length of time is unrealistic.

When working with children who display the failure-syndrome, be certain that tasks assigned are

1. Relatively short.
2. Completely understood by the child.
3. Fairly easy to accomplish (specifically, he knows the skill involved).

FEEDBACK

Furthermore, the child needs immediate feedback as to how he did. The failure-syndrome will be dispelled more quickly if feedback is immediate and positive. Should there be an error, sit down with the child and lead him back through the process—if possible allowing him to find and correct his own error—so that the paper receives a good grade. Do not penalize the child for the initial error.

It has been my experience that if the person working with the child is truly committed to helping the child, it is a rare situation in which the child cannot grasp the material. It is to be emphasized, however, that it frequently takes multiple sessions on the same topic for learning to occur, and once the child has the concept/skill it usually requires weekly to bi-weekly review of the skill for the child to retain it. After the skill is mastered, it may be used as a springboard to the development of other skills or ideas.

EVALUATION BY THE TEACHER

When you meet with defeat, your natural feeling is to "give up" —the same feeling the child has when he suffers defeat. If a child is not getting a concept, try as objectively as possible to evaluate what went on in the "teaching situation" by reflecting on these questions:

1. Was the child truly attentive? Did I provide for frequent and adequate oral feedback from the child to be sure he was really attending?
2. Was the task carefully planned so the child could follow the steps? Did I try to present too much information too fast?

3. Are there other ways to present the same material or task? Consider modalities—films, pictures, manipulative objects.
4. Was it simply a bad session because either the child or the person working with the child wasn't feeling good?
5. How many interruptions occurred during the "teaching situation"? LD children are easily frustrated by interruptions.

In general, once you have evaluated the defeat in this manner, you will feel better and be ready to try again the next day—perhaps using a different approach or materials.

INDIVIDUALIZING INSTRUCTION

In teaching today we hear again and again that we need to individualize instruction.

"Individualizing instruction" means designing a curriculum which maximizes the child's opportunity for learning. This implies a number of considerations, but there is one element we must clearly understand: *it does not mean every child will do a curriculum designed for him alone.* That would be an impossible teaching load. Such a practice also would not allow for the development of needed oral communication skills and social interaction skills. Individualizing instruction implies the teacher has

1. Assessed each child for his strengths and weaknesses.
2. Set up instructional groups designed to meet a common instructional need.
3. Selected materials appropriate to each child's needs both in terms of quantity and type.
4. Provided for a reward system which will help the child maximize his educational time and develop behavioral attributes necessary for successful living.
5. Provided for enrichment activities whereby faster students may pursue their interests.
6. Given attention to scheduling and room environment so as to provide students with the time, space, manipulative materials and atmosphere conducive to maximum learning. For the class that includes learning-disabled students, this mandates study periods when movement and noise are minimal.
7. Utilized sound principles of discipline.

Specific Learning Deficits

In the next few chapters you will be given suggestions for remediating a specific deficit. As you teach a child, keep in mind what his primary learning modality is. Visual and tactile learners need activities which require them to "look." An auditory learner often learns quicker by listening to you or a tape recorder.

5

How to Help Children Who Demonstrate Visual Perceptual Deficits

Visual perception is a process involving the receiving of visual stimuli, and interpreting them on the basis of past experience. Some children seem to have problems accurately perceiving objects. For example, when they view a cube ⌂ , they see 3 squares, or perceive no difference between an oak leaf and an ivy leaf. When they read, they do not discriminate between words of similar configuration. |dog| may be called |big| .

It is difficult to say how many children are plagued by visual perceptual problems, but from my experience in the field I would estimate as high as 25% of all school children in the primary grades have some degree of problem in this area. By third grade this percentage drops to about 10%. My conclusion is this: a great number of children with these problems either outgrow them or find ways to compensate for them. To illustrate, Bobby was 7 years old when he entered my second grade class. He could not say the *abc*'s without many gaps; he neither recognized nor wrote the letter *f*; copying anything from a book or the board was a total disaster; he read poorly and only because he had memorized the primer book word for word, and if he encountered a word he supposedly "knew" somewhere else, he was dumbfounded. The letters *b, d, s, p,* and *q* were confused in his mind, so he frequently reversed them in writing. Bobby was bright. By using various techniques described in this chapter, coupled with much teacher patience and encouragement, Bobby either outgrew his problems or learned ways to compensate for them.

Visual Perceptual Deficits   69

By the end of second grade he showed none of the behaviors noted at the start of the year.

HOW TO RECOGNIZE AND HELP CHILDREN
WHO HAVE VISUAL DISCRIMINATION DEFICITS

You can administer a simple teacher-made test for visual discrimination. Using the test that follows, ask the child to "find the two that are the same." (This test is not infallible due to the limited number of items and because results will vary according to age and experience of the child. However, an item missed indicates that a child may have a problem in this area. The more items missed, the more valid the test becomes.)

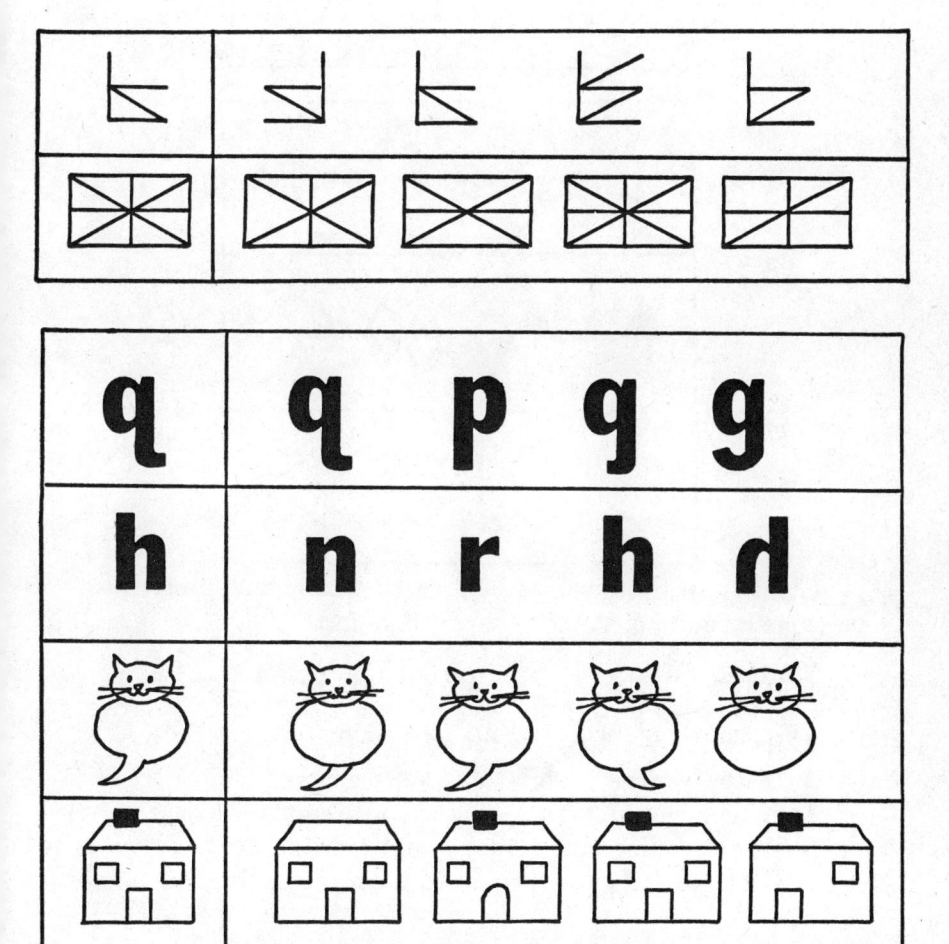

Visual Perceptual Deficits

Ask the child to "find the one that is different."

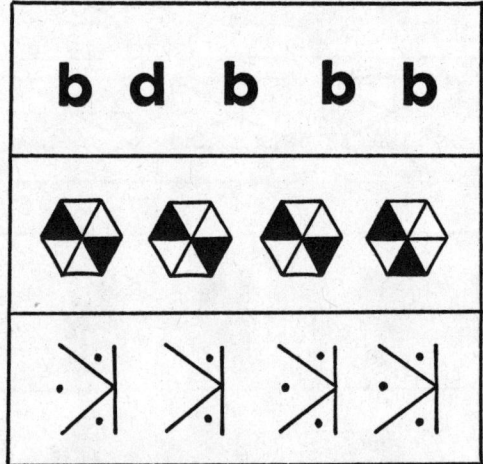

Children with visual perceptual discrimination problems will show one or more of the following symptoms:

1. Reversals—b for d, p for q, ƨ for s, ƨ for z, ɾ for j, Ɛ for 3.
2. Inversions—n for u, m for w, 6 for 9.
3. Letter confusion—h for n, r for n.
4. Sequencing problems—on for no, saw for was.
5. When reading aloud, they omit a word or group of words or insert a word or group of words, or they substitute a known

Visual Perceptual Deficits

word for the the printed word because the known word has the same initial consonant and configuration. To illustrate:

The horse was in the field is read as *The house was in the field*.

⌐▔▔▔▔▔▔┐   ⌐▔▔▔▔▔▔┐
| horse | | house |

6. Punctuation is disregarded.

If a child is having problems in the visual perceptual area, you should advise and urge the child's parents to take the child to an ophthalmologist—not an optometrist—for a complete visual examination. Send a note along with the parent such as the one which follows:

_____Name of child_____ is having difficulty in school. We have requested that you see him for a thorough visual evaluation to determine if he has any eye problems which would affect his school work.

We have noted ....

If you have noted any of the following difficulties add them to the letter to assist the physician:

1. Child complains of seeing double.
2. Child squints or blinks excessively.
3. Child closes one eye while working.
4. Child turns his head to one side while working or rests head on one arm while working.
5. Child complains of headaches.
6. Child becomes tired or sleepy (yawns) while reading.
7. Child complains of print being blurry or his eyes get red or itchy while using them; frequently rubs eyes.
8. Child is not able to copy from the board or frequently loses his place.
9. Child has difficulty hitting or catching a ball.

When the examination has been completed, the school should request a written report from the ophthalmologist. Sometimes physicians will make specific recommendations in terms of the child's seat assignment or conditions for use of corrective lens.

Educational intervention can begin before the physician's examination has taken place.

ACTIVITIES FOR REMEDIATION OF *B, D* CONFUSION

Technique 1. Have the child turn his hands this way:

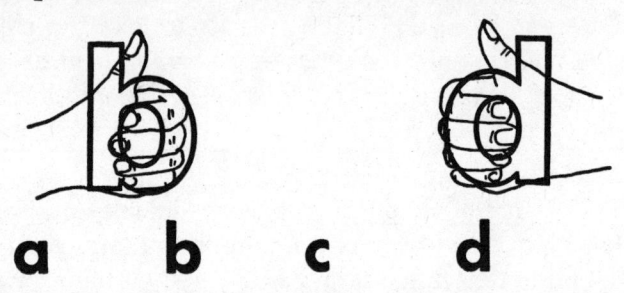

a   b   c   d

With a red pen draw letter on child's hands. Repeat this procedure daily for 5 days.

Technique 2. Ask the child to make a big *B*. If he does it correctly, point out that the little *b* turns the same direction, but the big *B* has 2 half circles on it. Repeat this procedure daily for 5 days.

Technique 3. With masking tape, fasten this on his desk. Leave on desk indefinitely.

Technique 4. Have child trace *b*'s, *saying b as he does each one.*

Repeat, tracing 5 times each day for 4 weeks without introducing or mentioning the *d*.

Technique 5. Have the child make *b* by rolling it in clay strips and bending it to *b* shape.

Visual Perceptual Deficits

Technique 6. Have the child locate all *b*'s in this sample:

j b c e d b f j
b t o b m l s b
r w b u b t l d

Then he colors each *b* red.

Note: Be certain to make each letter in the above exercise at least one inch high. Do not put *p* or *q* in exercise.

Technique 7. Ask child to locate all words in the following list that contain *b*:

bag   open   come   dog
        sit   bird
table   fix   pot   tub

When *b* is well-fixed, repeat same activities concentrating on the letter *d*.

REMEDIATION ACTIVITIES FOR P, Q

Note: Not to be used until b and d are mastered.

o p   q r

Technique 1. Trace p p p p p

5 times each day for 3 weeks, saying *p* as each is made.

Technique 2. Use clay practice, making and saying *p* as he does so.

Technique 3. Child locates *p* and colors each *p* from a list of 30 letters. You may include *b*, *d* in this list.

Technique 4. Child locates words containing *p* from a list of words.

REMEDIATION OF INVERSIONS

Adapt tracing, clay activities for *n, u, m, w.*

Use of sandpaper letters is recommended. Have child trace letter's direction by rubbing his pencil point over surface. Ask him to tell you which directions he is going as he does it.

REMEDIATION OF LETTER CONFUSION

Reteach formation of *h, n, r, n.* Point out the length of the bar in *h* as compared to *n.*

Point out that the *r* stops in midair and is not brought to the base line.

Use worksheets to reinforce skills taught.

Visual Discrimination Activities (After studying this sample, make your own)							
1. <u>a</u>	d	a	o	u	c	a	i	a
2. <u>d</u>	p	t	d	k	q	b	t	l
3 <u>h</u>	r	n	h	m	h	l	f	h

Sample from worksheet for inversion/letter confusion:

| 1. <u>n</u> | u | n | w | m | n | r |
| 2. <u>w</u> | m | w | w | m | w | m |

Visual Perceptual Deficits

Sample dot to dot activity worksheet

1 •

2 •
       6 •
   5 •   7 •
3 •

4 •   8 •

Find the letter you made in each of these words. ◯ it.

hat

ship

dish

ACTIVITIES FOR REMEDIATION OF SEQUENCING PROBLEMS

Technique 1. Place a masking tape arrow ⇨ on a child's desk. Have him hold the card with the word next to the arrow, so child can be sure to attack the word in left to right sequential fashion.

When a child misses a word, for example, *was*, ask him to spell the word to you so you are certain he is beginning with the right initial letter. If need be, draw word on a small card, putting the initial letter in red.

| Wa s |

Technique 2. If a child misreads a sentence, ask him to try it over. Insist on accuracy even if he must use his finger to point at each word.

Technique 3. Make worksheets requiring sequencing skills.

1. <u>on</u>	or	on	no	oh	on
2. <u>bad</u>	dad	had	bad	bed	
3. <u>saw</u>	saw	was	sam	saw	

Technique 4. Use configuration and color coding to assist a child who has repeated difficulty with the same word.

Sample: *Ten* is called *net*.

Child puts the first letter in red, second letter in green the third letter in blue and so on. Then he draws a high-low block around the word.

TEACH CHILDREN TO LOOK FOR PUNCTUATION

Reproduce, on dittoes, excerpts from the reading book. Where there is punctuation ., ?, !, leave space for the child to draw in a small stop sign. Sample:

Max was a big, shaggy, brown dog. He lived with Bill. Every day Bill took Max for a walk.
One day Max saw a fat hen. He chased her. She hopped to the top of a high fence.
Max barked and jumped at her.

becomes

Max was a big, shaggy, brown dog 🛑 **He lived with Bill** 🛑 **Every day Bill took Max for a walk** 🛑
One day Max saw a fat hen 🛑 **He chased her** 🛑
She hopped to the top of a high fence 🛑 **Max barked and jumped at her** 🛑

Have the child read this and, if necessary, similar activities *aloud,* being careful to come to a complete stop at each stop sign.

In later activities, the child can substitute a red mark for . ? !

Sally went to the store for new shoes . She got a balloon . She blew and blew . Pop !

HOW TO RECOGNIZE AND HELP CHILDREN WHO HAVE VISUAL FIGURE-GROUND DEFICITS

Visual Figure-Ground is the ability to focus one's attention on a given visual stimulus while other visual stimuli are also present. The

Visual Perceptual Deficits

child who experiences problems in this area may show any of the following symptoms

1. He loses his place frequently because his attention is diverted by all the other words or math problems on the page.
2. He is distracted from a task if there is any movement around him.
3. When the child looks at a picture he misses the central theme because his attention falls on some minor detail.
4. He is unable to copy from the blackboard.
5. He is unable to catch a ball. Because of the distraction of other objects in his visual field, his attention is drawn away from the on-coming ball.
6. He may complain he can't find an object, e.g., his pencil, on his cluttered desk because of the distracting stimuli from other objects.

There are several techniques that are helpful to a child with figure-ground deficits. If losing his place is the problem, the child should be encouraged to use a marker while reading. A 5" x 7" index card helps the child eliminate a portion of the distracting stimuli. If possible, this child will benefit from being seated at a carrel or in a part of the room where traffic is minimal. Marianne Frostig's *Program for the Development of Visual Perception*[5] provides excellent activities for helping children look for a central theme. You also can help children look for it by saying, "What things do you see in this picture?" If the child misses the central theme, encourage him to "Look for some more things" or say "What's happening?"

If a child's figure-ground problem is an inability to copy from the board, there are two techniques you may use. Try them according to the severity of the problem. *Technique 1:* If the child is inaccurate, assist him by underlining those words he has copied. Update your underlines as often as you can to keep his attention focused. *Technique 2:* If the above technique doesn't work, write the passage out for the child and allow him to cross out words as he copies them. If the child's figure-ground problem is an inability to catch a ball, say again and again "Keep your eye on the *ball*." He will improve.

---

[5]Marianne Frostig's *Program for the Development of Visual Perception* (Follett Publishing Co., 1973)—a kit of duplicable dittoes frequently found in school resource rooms and professional libraries.

ACTIVITIES FOR VISUAL FIGURE-GROUND DEFICITS

Use teacher-made or commercially produced design pictures such as this:

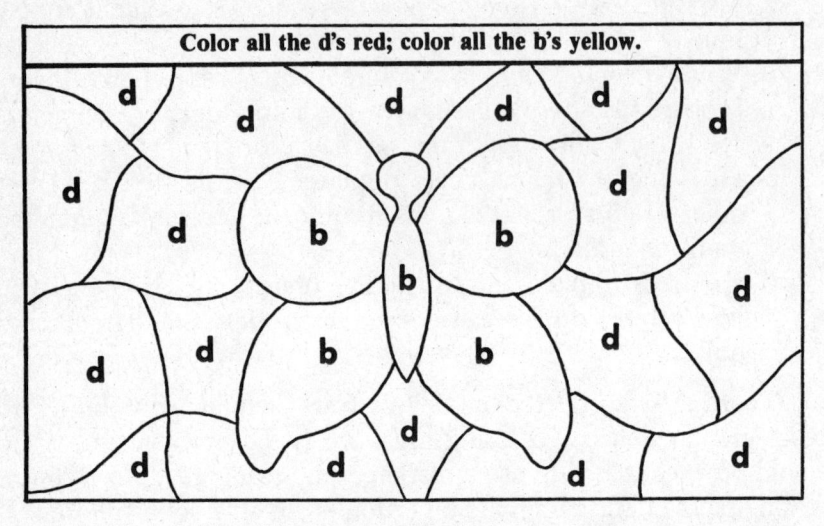

Color all the d's red; color all the b's yellow.

Buy or make activity sheets involving locating a word among other letters. Gradually increase degrees of difficulty as skills increase:

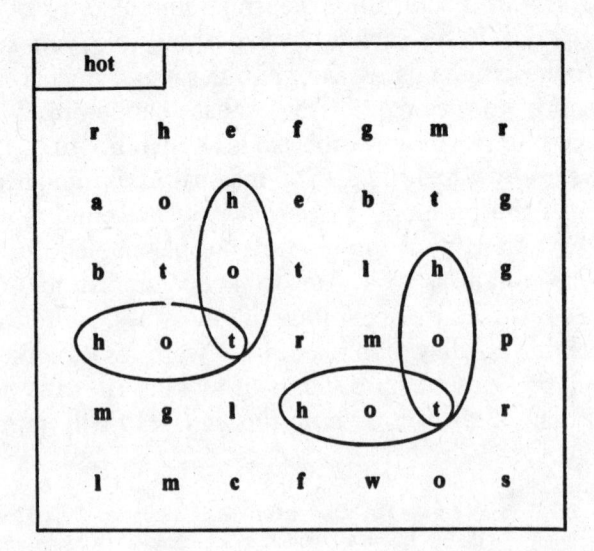

Visual Perceptual Deficits

The activity shown would not be suitable to a beginner.

Ask children to locate little words in big ones, e.g., *finger* has an *in*.

Use activity sheets where the child traces the direction of one line which intersects with others. In the following activity, ask the child to move his finger along the line beginning on the left side:

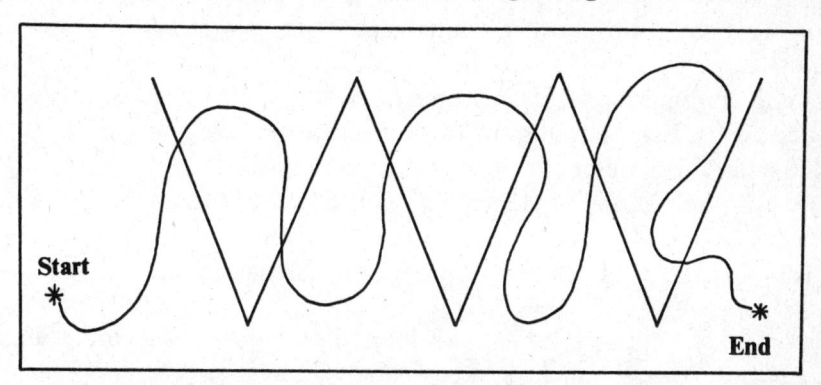

Scanning practice is another activity that is helpful to children with figure-ground deficits.

Commercially-made puzzles such as the following can be used. Ask the child to color all the triangles he can find:

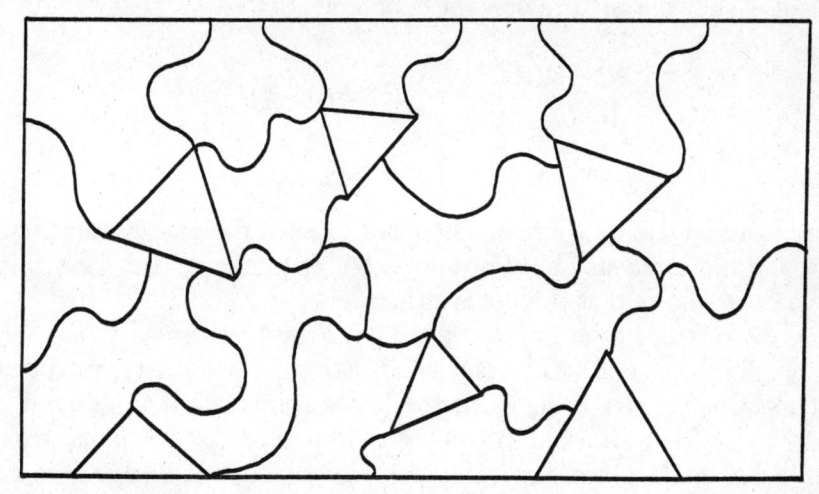

Older children should be asked to scan a page of printed material (a science book, social studies book can be used) for a given word or group of words.

Mazes, which can be commercially bought, are enjoyed by children and are helpful in remediation of figure-ground deficits.

HOW TO RECOGNIZE AND HELP CHILDREN WHO HAVE VISUAL CONSTANCY PROBLEMS

Probably the most obvious classroom symptom of a visual constancy problem is seen when a child comes to a word, letter or geometric figure which you thought he knew but he cannot get it because the print is different in size, shape, or color, or the angle of the symbol has been changed.

Another example of a child with a visual constancy problem occurs when a child looks at a picture of a 2-dimensional figure, but in his mind he cannot relate it to the 3-dimensional actual object. Thus, a picture of a cube may look like 3 squares to a child. Some children can recognize a picture of a square but when asked to name some objects that are square, the child cannot relate the concept of squareness to anything in his environment.

A final classroom example of this kind of problem occurs when a child is shown a picture of a set of objects such as

and is asked which is larger. The child looks at the pictures and says they're the same size but does not relate it to his real experience in which he knows that the cat is larger.

As before, I urge you to consult the Frostig materials. Above all, remember the child's feelings. He is frustrated when the type of print changes or the size changes. If you know a child can read dog but is puzzled by dog , tell him it is a g. Ask him what "d o g" spells. He'll probably get it. Often rewriting the material, such as a page of math problems, in larger print is all the child needs to be able to do the task.

Experiences involving 3-dimensional objects and talking about detail often help. Discuss the concept that objects which are close

Visual Perceptual Deficits

look smaller as they move away. For example, ask the child to think of a bus. Ask him if it is big or little. Ask him if the bus looks as big when it is two blocks away. End with "Did the bus shrink in size as it moved away or does it just look smaller?" Follow up this discussion by putting your finger two inches from the child's eye. Ask him to look at its size. Gradually move it away up to 5 feet, then ask the child what happened to its size. "Did it really get smaller or does it only look smaller?" Point out to a child that the illusion of distance occurs in pictures. A bright color in the lower portion of the picture with less bright colors in the background creates a feeling of distance.

See the sample worksheets for visual constancy deficits relating to letters, words or geometric figures.

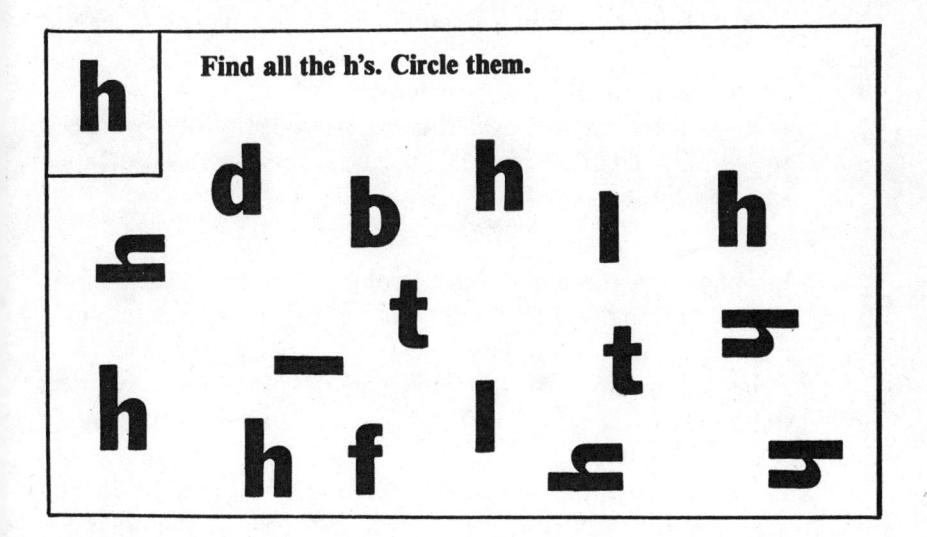

Find all the h's. Circle them.

Find the one that is the same.				
g	g	q	g	p
A	ʌ	A	A̵	A̵
m	n	ɯ	rr	m

The remediation of visual constancy problems requires a great deal of teaching time. The child having these problems can be helped very well by a trained aide or parent volunteer. This person can *provide experience* in looking at shape, size, color and position in space, and also *take time* to *discuss* what the child perceives (feedback). This is a one-to-one or very small group experience (no more than four children in the group). This person can help the child to look at an object in relation to other objects in the visual field. For example, let's say you ask a child to look at a picture of a tree and a house. The child can learn to guess the size of that tree by comparing it to the size of the house.

Children having visual constancy problems benefit by sorting tasks.

A box of buttons holds the potential for all types of sorting activities.

Day 1—Ask the child to sort by color.
Day 2—Ask the child to sort the same box of buttons by size.
Day 3—Ask the child to sort the buttons by the number of holes in the center.
Etc......

A box of geometric shapes (have a volunteer cut circles, squares, triangles and rectangles in a variety of colors and sizes) provides another manipulative sorting task.

Puzzles, commercially-made (less than 100 pieces), can be used to help children work by color. Teach the child to make the frame first, then work inward.

Finally, activities involving classification are helpful. Sorting pictures of animals into categories such as birds/fish/mammals requires the child to analyze the animal as to its characteristics.

HOW TO RECOGNIZE AND HELP CHILDREN WHO HAVE VISUAL MEMORY DEFICITS

The child experiencing visual memory deficits may show one or more of the following symptoms:

1. The child may claim he didn't see the directions.
2. The child cannot answer questions regarding a story he just read silently or he cannot remember what he saw in a film or TV story, even right after he saw it.
3. The child cannot remember a sequence of numbers accurately, for example, you ask him to copy a math problem and find 3149 is written 3194. The same jumble can occur when this child must copy a series of words from the board.
4. The child cannot remember how a word is spelled, even though he may have seen it just moments before and read it without error.
5. The child can recall only a limited number of visual stimuli once the stimulation stops.
6. The child is unable to recall where he stopped in a book if his attention is disturbed.

The aide or parent volunteer should work on a one-to-one basis with the child having visual memory deficits.

The geoboard can be of assitance in a visual program. These boards are commercially available or if you are handy a "can be made" pegboard can be obtained at a local lumberyard. You will need at least two, one for you and one for the student.

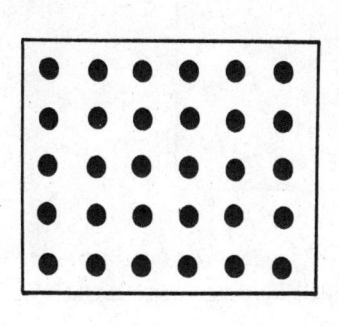

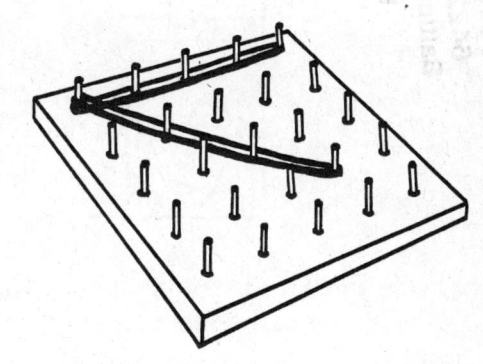

First, ask the child to reproduce designs just like the one you have made, while he is looking at your design. Teach the child to use the position of the pegs to decide where to attach rubber bands. As skills improve, increase the number of rubber bands from 1 to 2 to 3, etc. Next, you can buy rubber bands in a variety of colors to increase design complexity. Later, show him your board with one band; let him look 20 seconds, and then reproduce it from memory. If he is able to, try a 15 second looking exposure. Reduce it to 10 seconds next. If a child is able to do it this way, revert to 20 seconds and add another rubber band (2 designs to remember).

Parquetry blocks, tinker toys, blocks and Lego sets offer other mediums for teaching visual memory. You build a design. Allow the child to look a few moments then he tries to reproduce the design from memory. As the child improves he will need less and less time to fix a design in his memory.

Children love to play *concentration*. Make a board that looks like this:

On small cards put pictures of objects or words (you must make two cards for each object or word). Shuffle; place the cards on the board face down. The child turns up a card; then a second one. If it is a match, he keeps both cards. He continues to play as long as he makes a match. If the card he turns up doesn't match, the play then

Visual Perceptual Deficits

shifts to the next player. As the visual memory increases, you can increase the number of cards.

Using a tachistoscope, flash a picture, word or number sequence on a screen. Ask the child to reproduce the flashed stimuli.

Establish in the child the habit of looking for and reading written directions. This is best done by getting to the childs' side before he begins an assignment.

With the use of movies and filmstrips you can train children to remember a sequence of events. Show the film once and ask the child for the sequence. Write down each correct step. Reshow the film from the point where his memory failed.

The child who loses his place if his reading is disturbed can be helped simply. Let him put a penciled √ in his book. He can erase it later.

There are many things you can do to help the poor speller. Color-coding is most effective. You must use a consistent pattern. I use a system where the first letter is red, the second is blue, the third is green and the fourth is orange. The child can roll plasticene clay into ropes and form his spelling words with clay. You need to train children to look for special combinations, e.g., *th at* has two parts. Teach children to look for little words within big ones such as *and* in st*and*. Use spelling study sheets where a letter is missing, st __ p. Have the child supply the missing letter. Also ask the child to unscramble words; *ptos* is *stop*.

HOW TO RECOGNIZE AND HELP CHILDREN WHO HAVE VISUAL ASSOCIATION AND VISUAL CLOSURE DEFICITS

When presented with a major portion of an object or word, some children cannot supply the missing detail of that object or word. These are some examples of this type of deficit:

h __ l p   The child cannot supply the *e*, even if he reads the word easily when he sees the whole word.

The child cannot supply the missing wheel.

3 + ___ = 8   The child cannot supply the unknown, yet if we say 3 + 5 = ___, he gets the answer. This child may have difficulty with other fill-in-the-blank activities as well.

Some children just need experiences. For example, a child sees a cup and calls it a cup, but he cannot recognize that a mug is also a kind of cup.

Sometimes we find a child who has trouble manipulating mathematical symbols +, −, ×, and ÷ (he cannot remember which process the symbol stands for).

Some children can tell you a story verbally but are unable to put it in writing even if they know how to spell the words.

You have no doubt experienced the child who can read a set of directions but hasn't the foggiest notion what they mean. This is a visual association problem.

To help the child who cannot remember how to spell help, let him put the e in with a red pen.

The child who sees the wagon but cannot supply the missing part needs multiple drawing experiences with an adult at his side to help him look for visual detail. A parent volunteer can help. Worksheets like the examples shown help.

Put in the missing parts.

Visual Perceptual Deficits

Draw the missing part or parts.

When a child is having trouble with a fill-in-the-blank activity, have him read it to you first.

"The king wore a _____ on his head." Then you read it back to him; sometimes hearing someone else say the word triggers a correct response. If not, point to the key words, *king* and *head* and say "What is on the king's head"? Help the child make the correct associations.

When a child cannot get from 3 + ___ = 8, have him work with pictures until he has the concept.

In the case of a child who does not recognize that a ⌐⌐ and a ⌒⌒ are essentially "containers to hold liquids," a teacher can teach these concepts by bringing many containers (cans, jars, cups of various sizes/shapes) and a few items that will not hold anything, such as a book or a block of wood. The teacher then asks the child to find all the things that will hold water or juice. Discuss his choices after he completes this activity. Be certain the child uses the new words "container" and "liquid." Ask the child to name another container. Some children, especially children from culturally disadvantaged homes, need extensive language-visual experiences in order to develop visual associations. I remember being dumbfounded once to discover that only one child out of my class of 15 children knew what a toaster was. When shown a picture of a toaster, the other 14 called it a "Pop Tart." In Chapter 7, you will find a suggested program for

Language Development. It has a strong visual perceptual awareness component.

Working with children who have visual perceptual problems is a challenge, but it is also rewarding. By using the techniques and suggestions given in this chapter, you will see good results quickly.

6

How to Help Children Who Demonstrate Auditory Perceptual Deficits

Auditory perception is the process of receiving auditory stimuli and interpreting them on the basis of past experience. The child who has auditory perceptual problems experiences much frustration in school. He is often accused and even punished for "not listening." While it is possible that, at certain times, any given child may not be listening because of daydreaming, whispering, or passing notes; it is a matter of degree. This chapter concerns the child who habitually experiences auditory perceptual deficits. He may show one or more of the following symptoms:

1. He cannot follow directions given orally.
2. He does not comprehend material that has been presented orally—lectures and stories read to him.
3. He is not able to attend to a lesson presented in lecture form.
4. He is not able to do math problems presented orally, but he can do the same problems if they are written down.
5. He does not read phonetically, nor spell phonetically.
6. He is not able to discriminate likenesses and differences in sounds, particularly the short vowel sounds *e* and *i*.
7. He is not able to answer questions asked orally/takes an unusually long time to answer/or gives an inappropriate answer.

The child who consistently has auditory perceptual problems has more and more trouble in school as he grows older because

   a. The lecture technique is used with increasing frequency as the child progresses through the grades, and

b. Supporting visual stimulation (chalkboard samples, pictures) decreases as the child grows.

If a child is yelled at, punished or shamed for failure to "listen," the child may learn to hate the people who make him feel this way. The child with auditory problems is not ornery—he really cannot help the way he is. You can teach him ways to overcome or compensate for his deficits.

Learning to listen is harder than learning to use visual information obtained from books because

1. Visual information in the form of the printed word is permanent and can be reread if it isn't grasped the first time. The reader can even take time to refer to a dictionary if he hasn't a clear picture of word's meaning.

2. The reader can tell where one word ends and the next begins because of spacing. When we listen we normally get only one shot at the information (unless it's taped and can be replayed); therefore, we must rapidly process a word or group of words to get a mental picture. We must also be able to hear where one word begins and another ends. To illustrate what I mean, pretend you are giving directions. You say "Open your math book to page 110 and do problems 1 to 20", but to the auditorily handicapped child it sounds like "openyourmathbooktopage110anddoproblems1to20". This is confusing enough to the child, but if you also speak with a drawl, unusually fast or in very long sentences, the child simply gets only a partial and blurred message. If you have ever studied a foreign language, you have experienced the dilemma faced by the child with auditory perceptual problems. You were trying to make sense out of an auditory message given too rapidly and before you had sufficient familiarity with sounds to process them adequately.

There are many things you can do to help a child with auditory perceptual problems to learn to process auditory information more efficiently. The first thing to do is to ascertain that the child has normal hearing. Ask his parents to take him to a good audiologist for a thorough audiometric test. While waiting for the results of this testing use these suggestions:

1. Analyze the child's speech. If speech problems are present, the child should be receiving service from the speech therapist.

2. Seat the child near you in the classroom, so he can look directly at your mouth.

Auditory Perceptual Deficits

3. Reduce the rate of speed at which you talk—vary the tempo, loudness and intonation. How slow you must go will depend on finding the rate at which the child can process the auditory stimuli. It may be necessary to give instructions or presentation to the group at a normal speed and redo highlights on a 1:1 basis at a slow rate for the auditorily handicapped child.

4. Wherever possible, use visual stimuli to reinforce what you are saying, for example, oral directions can be summarized into written directions on the board.

5. Above all, make sure the child is attending as you talk. Get his attention gently with a touch or some form of mild direct address such as "Tommy, listen carefully. I'm going to say something important." When you say it, keep the irrelevant verbiage out. Reinforce the point by writing it on the board. Ask the child or children to keep notes.

6. Maintain a classroom environment that would be described as "quiet."

7. Determine which children have auditory perceptual problems and in what area their problems lie, then devise a systematic program for each child or small group of children to remediate that problem. An aide or a regular parent volunteer is essential to these children, and you will need to train that person in the auditory remediation techniques.

HOW TO RECOGNIZE AND HELP CHILDREN WHO HAVE AUDITORY DISCRIMINATION PROBLEMS

The child experiencing auditory discrimination problems may show one or more of the following difficulties:

1. An inability to tell the direction from which a sound is coming.
2. An inability to identify common sounds as to source, e.g., water running, a dog barking, a bell ringing.
3. An inability to discriminate between sounds such as *n/m; b/p; v/f*.
4. An inability to discriminate between short vowel sounds, e.g., *big* for *beg*.
5. An inability to hear likenesses (such as rhyming words) and differences in sounds.

We often assume that children have an adequately developed awareness of sounds and words. My experience as a teacher indicates this is not true. I was appalled several years ago to find that not a single child in my fourth grade class knew what "amazed" meant. They could not even think of a sentence using the word.

We need to increase the auditory awareness of children. We need to play a few games where the object of the game is for the children to determine where a sound is coming from. You can have the children close their eyes. Then situate yourself at a given point; say something and ask them to point in the direction from which the sound came. Devote some time to listening to sounds and trying to guess what caused them.

Several years ago I had the pleasure of working with Kenny, a child who had real "emotional" problems. According to his teacher, Kenny was beating up other children in his class and had tantrums during reading group. Kenny was the most frustrated 8 year old youngster I've ever seen. It came to pass that we learned his I.Q. score was 120, yet Kenny could not read anything above primer level. He was memorizing words. He had no idea each letter made a sound and these sounds could blend into words. Worse, when we began to work on sounds, we discovered he could not hear the difference in sounds; we had to teach Kenny to produce the letters *b, p, v, f, i, e, l, m* and *n* by methods normally used with deaf children. This training was productive, however. In one year, Kenny learned phonics so well that he was reading at grade level. The tantrums and aggressive behavior completely disappeared.

If you are working with a child who shows an inability to discriminate between letter sounds, there are three productive techniques for helping him develop letter-sound discrimination.

1. Teach the child to produce sounds just as a deaf person must learn them. Show the child where to place his tongue, teeth, lips, and how much air is necessary to produce the sound. Use a daily drill in front of a mirror (so he can check his lip, tongue and teeth placement) until sounds are mastered and come naturally.

2. Practice a given sound once the child has his lip, tongue and teeth placement correct, varying the speed:

p.p.p......p......p......p......p.p.p.

3. Introduce nonsense rhymes to reinforce production of the sound:

Peter piper picked a peck of pickled peppers (etc.).

Auditory Perceptual Deficits

Bo<u>bb</u>y <u>B</u>rontasaurus <u>b</u>it a <u>b</u>aby bat <u>b</u>one.
or
<u>V</u>era <u>V</u>iolet <u>v</u>iews <u>v</u>erandas <u>v</u>ery often.
or
<u>F</u>reddy <u>F</u>ox <u>f</u>ished <u>f</u>or <u>f</u>lounder <u>F</u>riday.

Especially we must teach the child the accurate production of the short vowel sounds. There are distinctive enough differences between lip placement that *a, o* and *u* are usually not difficult. It is the *i* and *e* that create confusion probably because the *i* sounds make an *e* sound, while the *e* sounds like the e in *egg*. These two sounds must be systematically taught and mastered by each child if the child is to ever be a good reader or speller. Some children will require a one-to-one relationship to learn this skill.

For an auditory training program to be successful children must be able to hear:

1. Individual sounds, and
2. Groups of sounds called syllables.

To illustrate, the child must be able to distinguish auditorily the difference in words such as *bed, bud, bid* and *bad*. Therefore, we have to teach auditorily handicapped children the skill of unblending: b*e*d becomes heard as b..*e*..d; this way the child hears clearly the vowel sound.

We must also teach children to listen for syllables or groups of sounds. In the primary grades we will teach children to count the number of syllables in a word. To do this:

Have children clap hands for each syllable:

<u>base</u> <u>ball</u> (2 claps)
<u>op</u> <u>pos</u> <u>ing</u> (3 claps)
<u>heard</u> (1 clap)
<u>ag</u> <u>gra</u> <u>vate</u> (3 claps)
<u>in</u> <u>tim</u> <u>i</u> <u>date</u> (4 claps)

Find or make word lists, varying the number of syllables, and do clapping activity at least five days in a row. Be sure to get enough feedback to make sure each individual can count the number of syllables. A ten item test at the end of five days can tell you which children still need help. You call the words. Give time enough for each child to mark down the number of syllables he heard. Repeat the word. Circulate to see which children need additional help learning this skill. The following test list may be used:

sat is fy	3	mon as ta ry	4
ban dit	2	lock	1
con cert	2	a cross	2
cu cum ber	3	im per so nate	4
ex cite ment	3		
milk	1		

There are other auditory discrimination activities to use. The following are types of activities most children need.

Tell the children you will call some words. If they hear *ball* in the word, they will clap. If they don't, they put a finger on their lips.

	Response
baseball	clap
cowboy	finger to lips
football	clap
ballgame	clap
ball field	clap
doorbell	finger to lips

Have them listen for "mis" in these words:

	Response
dismiss	clap
misplace	clap
mister	clap
resist	finger to lips
mislaid	clap

Make up other activities of this sort like *pay* using *paper, repay, daylight, payday* and *flavor*.

Children need rhyming activities. Spelling is greatly assisted through the use of rhyme.

The following lists can be used to teach the concept:

at	in	op	ub	et
cat	kin	mop	rub	bet
bat	pin	top	tub	get
sat	win	stop	stub	set
rat	tin	flop	scrub	net
fat	shin	drop	shrub	pet
that	din	shop	cub	let
flat	spin	slop	grub	met
mat				

Auditory Perceptual Deficits

<u>an</u>	<u>it</u>	<u>ot</u>	<u>ug</u>	<u>ell</u>
man	bit	hot	rug	bell
ran	sit	pot	hug	tell
pan	pit	spot	tug	spell
can	spit	shot	slug	fell
fan	fit	cot	shrug	dell
tan	flit	not	mug	sell
span	hit	lot	bug	shell
van	wit	slot		

<u>and</u>	<u>ink</u>	<u>ōne</u>	<u>ut</u>	<u>eat</u>
stand	sink	bone	cut	feat
hand	wink	stone	but	beat
sand	pink	shone	gut	seat
band	link	lone	hut	treat
land	slink	tone	mut	meat
	stink	cone	strut	
	think		put	

Use your own lists or use commercially-made lists for listening for similarity and difference in pairs of words.[6]

Begin with words that sound alike or different. Call out a pair. Ask the child to nod if two words sound alike and shake his head if they sound different:

cat—cat   top—pop
us—up   sink—sink
cone—coast   bone—boat
cut—cut   fish—wish
lead—led   trim—tram
lick—pick   soap—soup

Next ask them if paired words rhyme (nod) or do not rhyme (shake of head).

meat—feet   fun—sun
lake—make   like—bike
fin—chin   top—cap
cart—mop   took—take
bear—dare   can—man
come—ran   stand—band

---

[6]Additional samples of these types of activities may be found in *Helping Children Overcome Learning Difficulties*, by Jerome Rosher (copyright © 1975 by Jerome Rosner. Published by Walker and Company (720 Fifth Avenue, New York, N.Y. 10019). Obtaining Dr. Rosner's book will save numerous hours of lesson building.

Ask the children to determine if the following words begin with the same sound heard at the beginning of some:

swim	yes
snip	rose
jar	sock
rash	soil
spell	sour

Ask "Does the word begin with the *m* sound as in *mop*"?:

nose	came
mate	name
mix	most
time	money
maybe	seek

Ask the children to listen for a *m* sound on the end of a word:

home (nod)	land (shake)
came (nod)	wrist (shake)
open (head shake)	jump (shake)
wish (head shake)	Jim (nod)
swim (nod)	team (nod)

Make up word lists for *b, d, f, g* (as in *go*), *h, j, k, l, n, p, r, t, v, w, y, ch* and *sh* for additional practice.[7] Each type of activity should be repeated daily for five days.

HOW TO RECOGNIZE AND HELP THE CHILD WHO IS PLAGUED BY AUDITORY DISTRACTIBILITY OR AUDITORY FIGURE-GROUND PROBLEMS

Each of us is bombarded at any given moment by a multitude of sounds, yet most of us are able to pay attention to a few sounds and ignore others. There are some people, however, who have an inability to filter out extraneous noises. There have been cases where children complain they are distracted by their own breathing or heartbeat. In your classroom you may have a child who will complain about noise even though the room is not unduly noisy, or he may even cover his ears with his hands. Some children try to compensate for this

---

[7]If you wish to save time, consult Dr. Rosner's books for needed lists.

problem by cupping a hand behind the ear, or cocking the head to one side to focus on what the teacher is saying.

Just as the child with visual figure-ground deficits is confused by intersecting lines, the child with auditory figure-ground deficits is confused by intersecting or competing sounds.

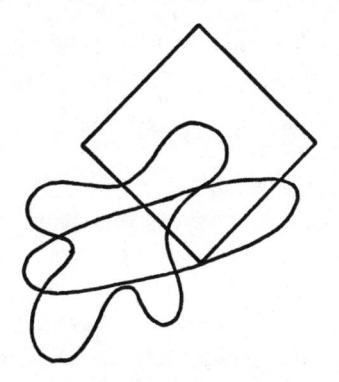

The obvious answer to helping the child who is bothered by noise is to let him work in a quiet place. Right? Wrong! This child desperately needs to learn how to attend to a speaker in the midst of conflicting auditory stimuli and how to attend to finishing his seatwork in a noisy room. Throughout his lifetime he will be bombarded by noises; he needs to learn to cope with them. You can help him.

First, the child must be aware he has a problem in this area. Once you are certain of this, have a 1:1 frank discussion of the problem with the child. You will carefully avoid fussing at him. A typical conversation might go something like this:

(Teacher has student in at lunch recess. Sit at a table—not at the teacher's desk. Share a package of chips or cookies to put the child at ease.)

Teacher: "Sally, I've been watching you and I'd like to share with you what I've noticed. You have shown me you know how to do these math problems, but you haven't been able to get your papers finished. Do you know why?"

(Listen to the child's responses. Don't argue with her. Hear her out, then say):

Teacher: "Sally, I think we can work together so you can get more work done, and it will be better work. I'm going to try to help you learn to work even if someone's bothering you or it's noisy. We'll make a game of it."

Next, explain the rules to her.

Teacher: "Sally, I'm going to try to bother you over the next couple of weeks. If I can, I win the game. If I can't, you win. We're going to put this baby food jar in your desk. I'll start you with ten marbles. Every time I bother you, you have to give me a marble. If I try to bother you and I can't, I have to give you a marble. I'm going to try to trick you into stopping your work and losing your place. Don't get mad, it's only a game. If you have ten marbles or more in five days, I'll give you some gum." (Sugarless, of course.) "Do you want to try it? You have nothing to lose because even if you lose all of your marbles you don't have to give me any gum, okay?"

When Sally is working go near her and drop a book. If she looks up, laugh and gently say, "I got you," and collect a marble. Repeat the identical distraction a few minutes later; most children won't look up again, so give the marble back this time. Say, "You won."

Next, try whispering the child's name while she's working. If she looks up, take a marble. Be sure to repeat the same distraction again in a short time period. Give a reward if the child does not look up.

Be alert to disruptions in the classroom such as someone coming through the door. If the child looks up, take a marble. Reward a marble if she doesn't. If assignments are completed early and accurately, reward the child. If the child gets distracted and fails to complete an assignment, take a marble.

The system you are using is called behavior modification. It works when applied diligently. In two weeks time, this child's ability to concentrate will be markedly improved.

Another technique that is helpful is teaching the child to listen to a recorded lesson on a tape recorder. Include background noise or music. Talk slowly and distinctly. Give the child some questions to answer. If the child can't get them, rewind and rerun the taped message until she can.

Lip reading and learning to focus attention on a speaker is also something this child must be encouraged to do.

HOW TO RECOGNIZE AND HELP THE CHILD WHO HAS AUDITORY MEMORY DEFICITS

Auditory memory is the ability to retrieve information which has been received via the hearing channel. The primary-aged child should be able to remember and respond to verbal directions up to three parts. For example, you should be able to say "Put your pencil

Auditory Perceptual Deficits

where you can find it; slide your chair under your table; and line up quietly" and expect that the child will carry out all directions. Children should be able to remember major facts from a story just read to them and be able to answer questions regarding the selection. A child in grades one to three should be able to memorize short poems of up to 6 lines and songs of 6-10 lines. A child by the age of seven and a half should be able to count to 100 by rote with no errors, should say the alphabet with no errors, should know his address and phone number, and the days of the week and the months of the year in sequential order. Children by the end of grade 4 should know their basic addition, subtraction, multiplication and division facts by memory. If a child is unable to do these things, he may have an auditory memory problem. He needs auditory memory training.

The child experiencing auditory memory deficits can benefit a great deal from auditory memory training activities. The following samples are aimed to increase the child's ability to listen for directions and to listen for detail.

Give each child a worksheet. Have each child place his finger by #1. Tell them you are going to read a rhyme. They will *circle* each "thing" mentioned in the rhyme. Draw a circle on the board to demonstrate. Read slowly.

> Jack and Jill went up the hill
> To get a pail of water.
> Jack fell down and broke his crown
> And Jill came tumbling after.

After you read the rhyme, walk around and give immediate feedback. If a child did it right say "Yes," "Great," "Super," "Good" or "Fantastic." If they missed, repeat the rhyme. Demonstrate what was wrong.

Child's #1 looks like this on worksheet:

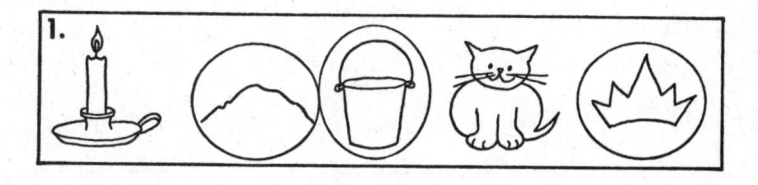

In the next rhyme you may ask that they mark all the items mentioned but instead of a circle ask them to "put an X on each thing mentioned."

In other examples vary the directions "put a box around," "put a line under," "put an X with a red crayon on the first thing mentioned in the poem and put a circle with a black crayon on the last item mentioned." The latter type direction is not to be used until students are proficient (mastered) in easier, less complicated directions such as "circle the first thing mentioned."[8]

For the older child, nursery rhymes lead to listening for details in a short story. The work sheet will not be pictures, but written questions regarding who did what, where they did it and when or why they did it. For example, the Paul Bunyan tales seem to fascinate youngsters. Read a short selection. Give a worksheet with questions similar to the one that follows:

Put an X on each correct statement.

____ Paul Bunyan was a logger/lumberman.
____ Paul Bunyan came from a family with seven children.
____ Paul Bunyan was very strong.
____ Paul Bunyan loved to sing.
____ In this story, Paul Bunyan had a Blue Ox.
____ Paul Bunyan ate ten pies at McDonalds.

ACTIVITIES FOR INCREASING AUDITORY MEMORY

Give each child a worksheet like this:

_____Name

1.   6.
2.   7.
3.   8.
4.   9.
5.   10.

---

[8]There is a very excellent book available with complete lesson plans and worksheets. Your resource room or professional library may have it. It saves hours of lesson-development time. Selma E. Herr's *Perceptual Communication Skills* (Los Angeles, CA: Instructional Materials and Equipment Distributors).

Auditory Perceptual Deficits

Say, "I'm going to read four numbers to you. Hold your pencil in the air until I say 'Go.' I will read the number sequence. You will then write what you think I said. Try to make a picture of each number—see it in your head—as I say it."

Read the sequence slowly. Circulate. See how they did. Give feedback "Right," "Fine," "You got it," etc. If a child missed, tell him what you want him to do again. This time when you tell him he is to imagine a number in his head—give him a clue. Raise your finger. Write in the air a 5, 2, 3 and 9 so he gets the idea of how to make a mental picture. Make up sequences such as these:

1. 2019
2. 6399
3. 1379
4. 2468
5. 4253
6. 2130
7. 8541
8. 3596
9. 2109
10. 8210

As the children get better at remembering, use the same kind of worksheet but increase the sequence difficulty by giving five digits, or adding processes, such as $2 + 0 + 1 + 9$ or $6 + 3 - 4$, etc.

Another excellent type of activity for increasing auditory memory is having the child learn to retell stories involving remembering sequences such as in "The Gingerbread Boy," or "Three Billy Goats Gruff." Even older primary children can be conned into remembering such sequences if they are rewarded for mastery by being allowed to go as a storyteller to a kindergarten class.

Most children like music and little children like musical sequences such as Hokey Pokey. They enjoy learning fingerplays such as the "Eensey Weensey Spider." Older children enjoy direction-sequence games such as "Turn to page 12, find the second paragraph. Write the fifth word" and these are excellent activities in terms of carry-over in daily direction following.

HOW TO RECOGNIZE THE CHILD WITH AUDITORY ASSOCIATION AND AUDITORY CLOSURE PROBLEMS

The child needs to be able to recognize and complete parts of the whole from a partial stimulus. He also must be able to integrate previously learned material with new material received auditorily. For example, if you said "A banana is yellow, a tomato is _____," most children quickly supply the missing word *red*. The child with association problems will not respond or will take a long time responding because he cannot process the question and relate it to previous experience. Another example of this kind of problem occurs when you ask the child to compare two items for likenesses or differences, as when we ask children to compare two poems or questions such as "How are a bus and a plane alike?" In math if you say "Is nine more than or less than four?", the child is not sure, but when presented the same question visually:

Which is more? | 9
Circle the number | 4
that is more

the child gives a correct response. The child with auditory association problems has trouble with cause and effect relationships.

You say "Jan's dog has been run over. Why is she crying?" Most children will say "Because she's sad," "Because she'll miss him," but the child with association problems may say "I don't know" or give an incorrect response such as "Because she'll get in trouble." Using this example you might go on to ask "What will happen next?" Most children will say, "She'll bury the dog" or "She'll get a new puppy" but the child with association problems is unable to make a correct association.

In the area of behavior these children have difficulty understanding why something happens. For example, you may say "If you talk, you will get your name on the board and then you lose your recess." The child talks but when he loses his recess he says, "Why can't I go out?" He really did not understand he'd lose the recess if he talked. But you must carry through with keeping him in or he'll never make the association.

Auditory closure refers to the ability of the child to blend sounds into words, to blend words into sentences of correct meaning, to use correct verb tense, and to blend ideas into paragraphs. Some children can learn phonics perfectly looking at
"toast" and saying
t ... ō ... s ... t, but be unable to close it to "tost" and get the mental picture of a piece of toast.

Another example of this situation is found in sentence structure. The child wants to say "I would like to try that" and it comes out "Me wants to do that." In this case the child knows his mind but he can't remember how his request should be phrased.

A great deal can be done for all children in the name of auditory

Auditory Perceptual Deficits

association. In many cases, in my opinion, children have problems in this area simply because no one has time to talk with them. Mom and Dad are busy working and are too tired at night or on weekends to talk, older siblings consider younger ones to be an "itch" which is to "go away," and TV, the modern child's main source of auditory stimulation, talks to kids but offers no opportunity for feedback from the child. The modern child suffers from being talked *to* instead of talked *with*.

I encourage teachers to take time to listen to children as they discuss how they feel about experiences. Share your experiences if they relate to the child's. If a child shares an experience with you that is a fairly universal one, sometimes class time should be devoted to discussing these common experiences and using them for drawing conclusions as to cause and effect and probable outcome. For example, one day Jan came to school very upset. It seems she had broken a vase. Her parents had already gone to work so they did not know yet. I shared with her that my daugher, Jakki, had done the same thing. She asked what kind of punishment Jakki got. The class heard this and everyone got involved. Several kids told experiences they'd had but we also talked about parents' emotions "why the broken vase would upset them—an heirloom, expensive, etc.," and we talked about the different consequences that could befall the child who broke the vase. Jan's punishment was fairly moderate, but she was prepared with a foreknowledge of possible punishments, mild to severe. She felt her punishment was fair.

There are innumerable kinds of association activities. Here I'll skim the surface. Selma Herr's book gives many activities.

With young children you may give a worksheet of pictures such as the example here.

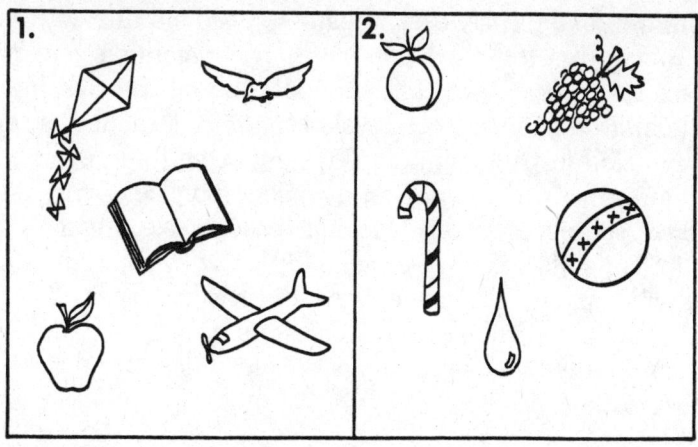

In number 1 you might say "Circle all the pictures of things that can fly." In number 2, you might say "Put an X on all the things that taste sweet." Some children may need the actual tasting experience.

For older children, you might use strictly auditory stimulation such as "Which is loudest: a shout, a whisper or a scream?", or "Which goes faster: a snail, a cat or a horse?"

Children need experiences in classification. You can play games such as rhythm where they must give additional words that belong to the same group. For example, if the group is Birds, each person adds the name of a kind of bird: quail, robin, turkey, pelican, until someone cannot think of one in the time allotted.

Discussions, maybe even one a day routinely, such as follows, can produce great learning. Say "I'm thinking of three things: a cracker, a piece of toast and chili. How are they alike?" Discussions which begin "What would you do if ... ?" make excellent spring-boards. For example, "What would you do if you found twenty dollars?" Children's answers can be amazing!

Riddles are a favorite. You start it. Maybe allow one riddle a day, but also be sure the children get the association.

"What has a horn and gives milk?" The milktruck must be explained to modern children who were born after the day of the icebox or milkman.

"I'm thinking of" games are fun. "I'm thinking of a word that rhymes with bed. It is a color. What's the word?" Allow the children to take turns at this game. Older kids love to play a form of this game called 20 Questions. A student may say "I'm thinking of a famous building." The children then get to ask any question that can be answered with "yes" or "no." On the basis of their questions—no more than 20—they win the game if they guess the answer.

Children like to play closure games. It's done this way. You say "I'm thinking of a three syllable word. It's something you can eat. Clues are *cu ... ber*". The children guess the missing syllable *cum*.

All children need help to develop sentence structure, a sense of tense, and skill in paragraph development. One thing we should all be alert for is that students answer questions—oral and written—with a *complete* sentence. When teaching tense, make a game of it by calling it "Time Machine." Ask the children to develop sentences that show it will happen, it is happening and it has happened. You can do this by making a cardboard time machine with three knobs: past, present and future. The prop seems to help children find the subject more interesting.

Earlier in this book I said I felt the most important facet of teaching is *feedback*. As I close this chapter, I again urge you to actively seek verbal feedback from children for a substantial portion of each school day. A colleague of mine has developed what I consider a very worthwhile system of verbal feedback. At the end of each day, he leaves 15 minutes. Randomly he selects students to discuss "What did I learn by coming to school today?" The way the question is phrased, it allows for learning outside of the classroom. The teacher talks in depth with 3 or 4 kids about something they learned.

If Sammy said "I learned about whales" it didn't end there. Sammy was asked to deliver a mini-review of "all about whales." This teacher made sure in the span of a week that he had called on each child to do the mini-review at least once. This review had a carryover to the lessons. The kids paid closer attention because they liked "shining" at mini-review time. The teacher rewarded especially good reviewers a cookie or some token of appreciation. These 15 minute discussions gradually expanded to 20 then to 30 minutes with student-teacher exchange of ideas. It was the finest display of teacher-student learning I've experienced. I urge you to try it.

7

Helping Children Who Demonstrate Deficits in Body Awareness and Motion Control

Perception is the process of receiving visual, auditory or tactile stimuli. In the brain these stimuli are interpreted, categorized and related to previous experience. This represents "input." When a child must make a physical or motor response, we are dealing with "output." Some children accurately perceive. They call a circle by its name; say it is round and are able to relate its quality of roundness to other objects such as a ball, globe or orange, but when asked to draw one they come out with ovals or with figures that are not closed properly. This is one example of a motor deficit. In previous chapters we've discussed perceptual deficits and remediation of the same. In this chapter we will discuss body awareness and the development of general motor skills.

A large percentage of the children who are experiencing learning problems will also be poorly coordinated. Some authorities in special education have suggested that by improving a child's movement skills you can also help him in reading and math. Other authorities disagree. My own view is this: Movement skills are important to the well-being of each child and therefore should be taught to all children. I strongly recommend at least 30 minutes a day be directed to activities that develop motor skills. A strong body (physical fitness, good coordination) is a definite asset. It's also not a bad idea for the teacher to participate in many of the activities to stay physically fit also.

HOW TO LOCATE CHILDREN WHO NEED DEVELOPMENT OF SPECIFIC MOTOR SKILLS

While all children can benefit from a physical fitness program, certain children will need additional activities and help. It is simple to locate these children. By mid-first grade children should be able to

1. Balance on one foot for 10 seconds (test both feet).
2. Hop a distance of 15 feet on one foot.
3. Skip a distance of 15 feet.
4. Draw a line connecting two dots, regardless of whether the line is vertical, horizontal or diagonal.
5. Cut along a line with scissors.
6. Tie a shoelace or ribbon in a bow.
7. Follow a visual target with both eyes moving together.
8. Repeat a pattern tapped 2 times with right hand, 2 times with left, 2 right, 2 left and so on. Tap should be continued at a steady tempo with no lulls.
9. Copy a circle, closing it and having it clearly round, not oval. Leave design so he can copy it. This is not a memory test.
10. Make a plus sign +.
11. Produce a square.
12. Draw a triangle.
13. Copy a divided rectangle.

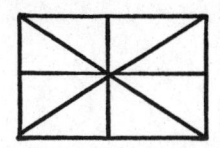

It is easy to test the above skills. In addition, you will want to observe whether each child moves about without undue clumsiness, runs and walks smoothly, and produces written work neatly and legibly.

DEVELOPING A PROGRAM OF GROSS MOTOR SKILLS FOR ALL CHILDREN

As I said I feel at least 30 minutes daily should be devoted to physical skills development for all children. In addition to this 30 minutes time period, children with deficits in any area you tested should have help from a parent or aide to learn the skill needed. If a parent or aide is not available, upper-grade students can successfully assist in the motor program if they understand what the skill is, how to do it, and conscientiously help the younger child to perform the skill correctly.

You will need some equipment. The following list is suggested:

1. A balance beam. If worse comes to worse, you can use 2 bricks or 2 concrete blocks to suspend a 12 foot piece of lumber across.
2. Balls, tennis size to dodge ball size. Try to obtain a 7 inch diameter foam rubber ball.
3. Six old bicycle tires.
4. A scooter board. This can be simply made. Take an 18" x 18" board, cover it with carpet, and attach dolly wheels to the bottom (one per corner).
5. Jump ropes, several lengths.
6. A wooden ladder.
7. Bean bags.
8. A board 3' x 3' with five circles cut out to toss bean bags through.

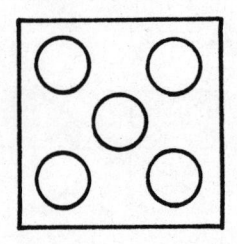

9. Mats or a carpeted area (carpet tacked down so it doesn't slip).
10. Hoola hoop.

Before beginning a lesson, explain the lesson task to the participants. Demonstrate the skill youself, if possible. Remind the children there will be no horseplay. (I exclude children from participation that day—they sit on the rug—for horseplay. Safety must be a foremost consideration). Only one child does a skill at a time, so the adult or child supervisor can watch to assure it is correctly done. If flubbed, the child is asked to repeat it. Hopefully he will achieve the skill in two or three attempts. Every time a skill is correctly performed, give verbal commendation right then.

Balance Beam Activities

The following are some lessons which can be used with the balance beam:

Activity 1. Without shoes, with balance board 3" off of the ground, walk the length of the balance beam with a heel-to-toe gait. Teach children to walk its length with eyes straight ahead (feet feel for the board). This can be done if the adult puts her hand 2 feet ahead of the child's eyes. The child is to look at the teacher's hand, not at his feet. If a child is unable to steady himself on the beam, allow him to hold hands with someone walking beside the beam. With repeated trials the child will need less and less assistance.

Activity 2. Walking the balance beam as described above, add on a second skill. Put a bean bag on the child's head. The object is to keep from dropping the bean bag while walking the plank.

Activity 3. Have the child walk forward on the balance beam heel-to-toe but bouncing a large rubber ball on the floor beside the beam as he goes.

Activity 4. Place obstacles on the balance beam. For instance, a bean bag every 15". The aim now is for the child to step over each bean bag without slipping off the board.

Activity 5. Have the balance board 3" off the ground. This time the child stands sideways on the board. Moving his leading foot first, he side steps across the board. When he reaches the end he returns by using the other foot to lead.

Activities Using Old Tires

Activity 1. Arrange tires thusly—touching:

Child stands on tape flat footed. Jumping on both feet in rabbit fashion, he works his way to the end. As he hits in the center of each tire, his foot should not touch the tire rim.

Activity 2. Place tires this way:
Jump rabbit fashion.

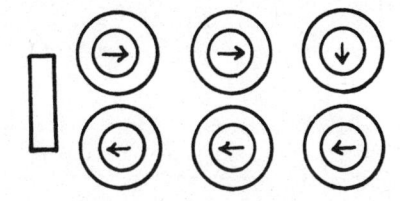

Activity 3. Place tires thusly. As the child puts his left foot forward, it goes into the left tire. Then the right foot into the right hand tire. Alternate feet to the end.

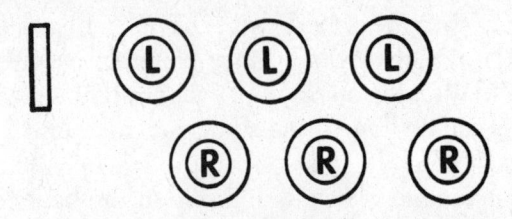

Activity 4. You need 6 bean bags. Place tires in a row. Have the child stand on tape and try to toss one bean bag into the center of each tire beginning with the closest one.

Activity 5. You need a large bouncy rubber ball. Place tires in a row. Walking beside the row, bounce a ball inside each tire, catching it between bounces.

Activity 6. You need tires and a jump rope.

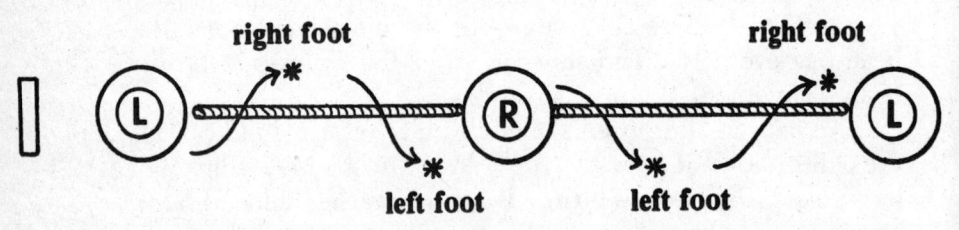

Child jumps into the first tire on the left foot. Right foot leaves the tires and is put on the left side of the rope. Now the left foot finds its way to the right side of the rope. The right foot lands in the second tire. The left foot then is put on the right hand side of the rope. The right foot crosses over. The left foot lands in the center of the last tire.

Activities Using a Ladder

Activity 1. Jumping flat footed, the child jumps between the rungs of a ladder.

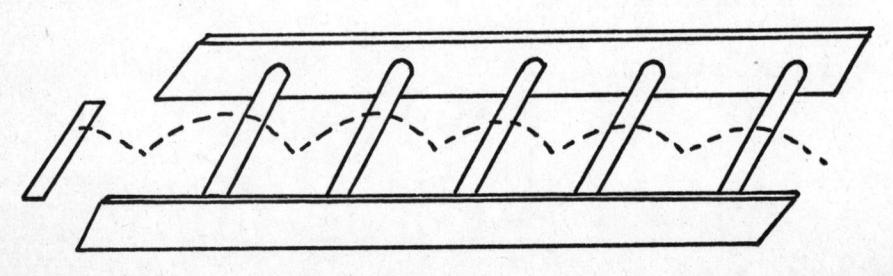

Deficits in Body Awareness and Motor Control

Activity 2. With ladder flat on the floor, the child crosses the ladder without shoes, stepping on each rung.

Activity 3. With the ladder flat, the child walks beside the ladder bouncing a ball between the rungs.

Activity 4. With the ladder turned on one side, the child crawls in and out between rungs.

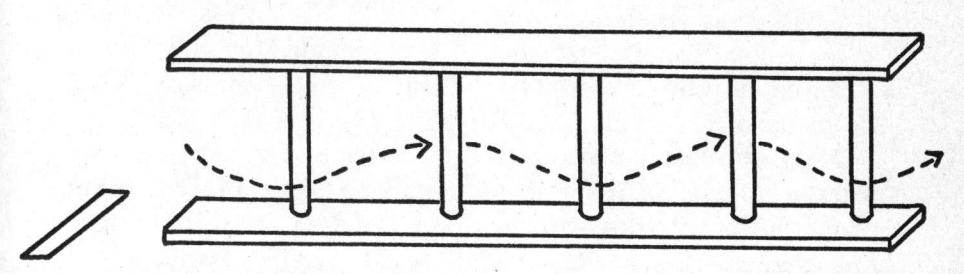

Activity 5. With the ladder elevated on concrete blocks, the child walks without shoes up the rungs, balancing himself with his arms or with help from a friend.

Activity 6. With the ladder flat, the child steps between rungs, varying foot—left, right, left, etc.—turns and returns, moving in a lively fashion.

Activities Using Balls or Bean Bags

Throwing and catching—vary the type of ball or bean bag and distance from the target or catcher. Target can be a waste paper basket or a loop of heavy paper (similar to a basketball hoop) attached to a wall (use a foam rubber ball).

Bean bags and tape can make an obstacle course:

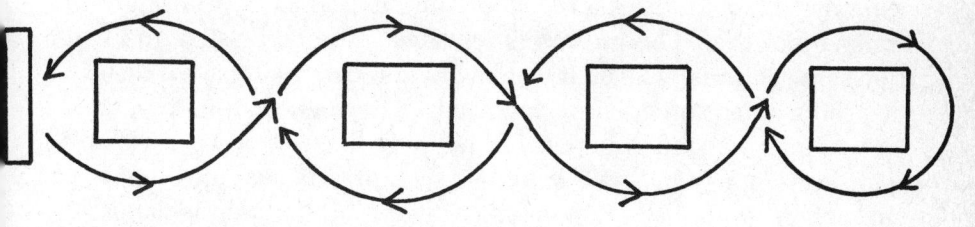

Crawling, hopping or walking heel-to-toe, the child can move in and out between the bean bags.

Other Activities

Jump ropes can be held taut by two students at various heights from the floor. Depending on the height, activities can vary from slithering under it by propelling yourself by the toes, to crawling, to jumping over it.

A **scooter board** is a very necessary piece of equipment. It helps children develop strength in the arm muscles. Lying on their belly across the scooter board, the child propels himself by the use of his arms only along a tape-highway or from one point to another. The pathway may run around obstacles.

The **Hoola Hoop** is great when used by an individual child, but it also can be used by three children. Each child holds onto the hoop with one hand. They run in a circle pulling gently against each other.

Other exercises for arm muscles include push-ups. Lying belly down, the child raises his chest and tummy off the floor by the use of his arms. Begin with three and work up. Children also need to work out on overhead rings or the bars if these are available at your school. Tug of wars with a rope are good for arm muscles and are fun also.

Mat activities can include rolling side-to-side; turning somersaults, playing wheelbarrow (an arm builder—one child walks on his hands while another child carries his legs like the handles of a wheelbarrow); lying on the back and pretending to ride a bicycle.

In addition to the above activities, children should run, walk, jog and play games such as dodge ball and kickball. For older elementary children add baseball, soccer or frisbee (the frisbee game follows the same rules as baseball. Instead of hitting a ball, the batter throws the frisbee and runs the bases). Relay races and competition add a variety in that the directions can allow for skipping, jumping and hopping, as well as walking.

The fast side step is a difficult but good activity. Standing sideways the child takes a big step with his lead foot. He brings his trailing foot over. The process is repeated faster and faster. You will find some children who do it well in one direction, but have difficulty returning when the opposite foot leads. They benefit from practice.

Animal walking is beneficial; hopping like a kangaroo; walking with arms down and swaying from side to side like an elephant; running on tip-toe and flapping arms like a bird all develop muscle tone. You should also include bending and stretching exercises.

DEVELOPING A PROGRAM FOR BODY AWARENESS

Children need help understanding the functions of their body. They need to be able to locate various body parts. They should be able to judge whether they can manipulate their body through certain amounts of space. Children need to be able to relate the placement of objects to space. They should clearly know their right from their left. They should be able to identify certain things merely by feel. The activities that are suggested here should be repeated every year of elementary school because they are important.

You need to give health lessons on the body's systems: skeletal, muscular, circulatory, digestive, nervous and excretory.

Children need to be able to identify various body parts. Have children lie on the floor and close their eyes. Ask them to point to their left foot, right ear, thigh, abdomen and chest. They need to learn words like abdomen.

Using large sheets of butcher paper, have a child lie down; *help* another child trace with a crayon around his friend. Then ask the first child to take his body tracing and add eyes, nose, mouth, hair, etc.

Play "Do as I Do" game. The teacher or a child strikes a pose. All of the other participants try to imitate it.

Teach children to draw faces. Start with having them draw a large oval. Next they put a light dot in the center (later this dot is erased and a nose is added). They place two dots slightly above the mid-dot (nose). They will be the eyes.

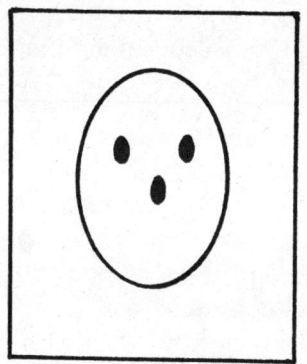

Have the children feel their own heads. How much space is above the end of your nose? How much space is below? Where are the lobes of your ears in relation to the end of your nose?

Looking at a partner, have them practice drawing eyes, looking for visual detail.

The eye is almond shaped. Bring almond nuts in. Trace around them. Fill in the eye detail of the circle in the middle, touching both the top and the bottom.

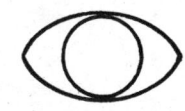

Add the pupil and point out that in the colored section of the eye we often can see small lines and flecks of a darker color.

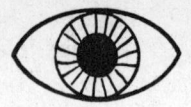

Show children how to add lines above and below the eyes.

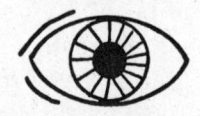

Add eye lashes, longer, curlier ones on top and shorter lashes at the lower rim.

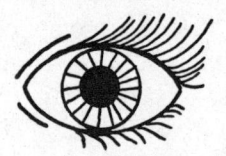

Teach the drawing of noses and mouths.

You may be saying "I'm no artist." But you too can learn by standing in front of a mirror, looking at your own mouth and drawing. What is the shape of the upper lip? Lower lip? Are there lines?

Drawing hands, feet and arms all provide opportunity for increased visual perception (seeing detail) and development of the child's concept of his own body.

Children need to be able to judge whether they can manipulate their body through a given amount of space.

Build mazes using tape and odd placement of classroom furniture. Require the child to manipulate his way over, under, around and between the furniture as he follows a taped path. Use and teach words over, under, around and between.

Scatter beans on the floor leaving only tiny, clear patches for feet at negotiable intervals. Ask the children to work their way across without toppling over (balance with arms) or stepping on the beans.

Children need experiences in reproducing patterns.[9] This can be done with teacher-made dittoes such as seen here:

---

[9]Again the Frostig kit for Development of Visual Perception offers many already prepared worksheets which can save you time.

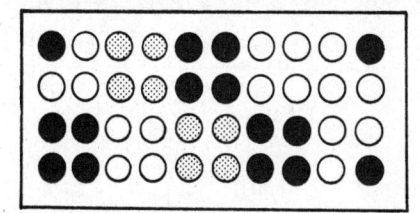

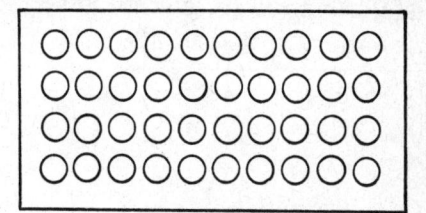

Deficits in Body Awareness and Motor Control 115

The child looks at the design on the top row (below) and copies them into the blanks on the bottom row, or other types of design copying can be used.

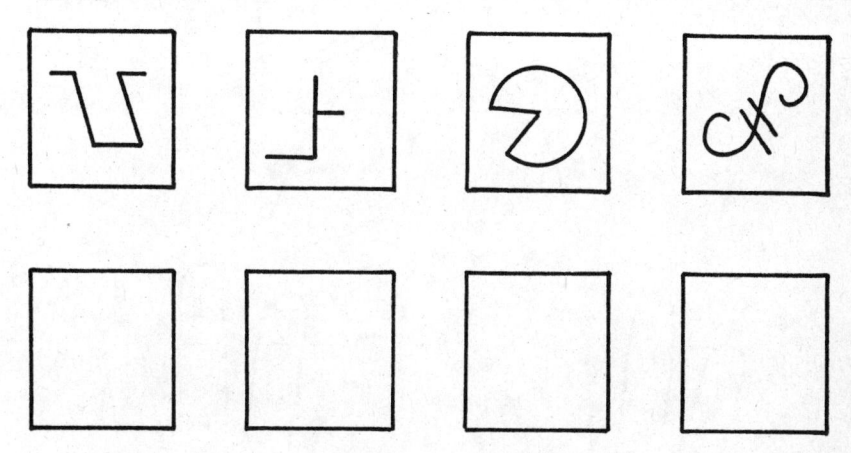

Children must have multiple cutting experiences. Have the children begin with various kinds of lines—straight, wavy, circular and angles. Later use objects such as geometric figures or simple objects, later intricate cutting of figures.

Jacks and darts are games which help children learn to judge position in space.

Origami or Japanese paperfolding is an excellent way to teach position in space, as well as develop muscle control.

Dot-to-dot activities are good for children.

Teach right and left concept thoroughly. I tell most children "you write (rit) with your right (rit) hand." Be careful to tell your lefty's this does not apply to them. Play games like Loopy Loo.

Use drawing activities to help the child identify right and left. Have a child draw his hands, palms down or palms up. He can trace around them and add details with your help. This activity requires children to really look at their hands. When all four pictures are done, mix them up and ask the child to identify which is his left hand? Right hand?

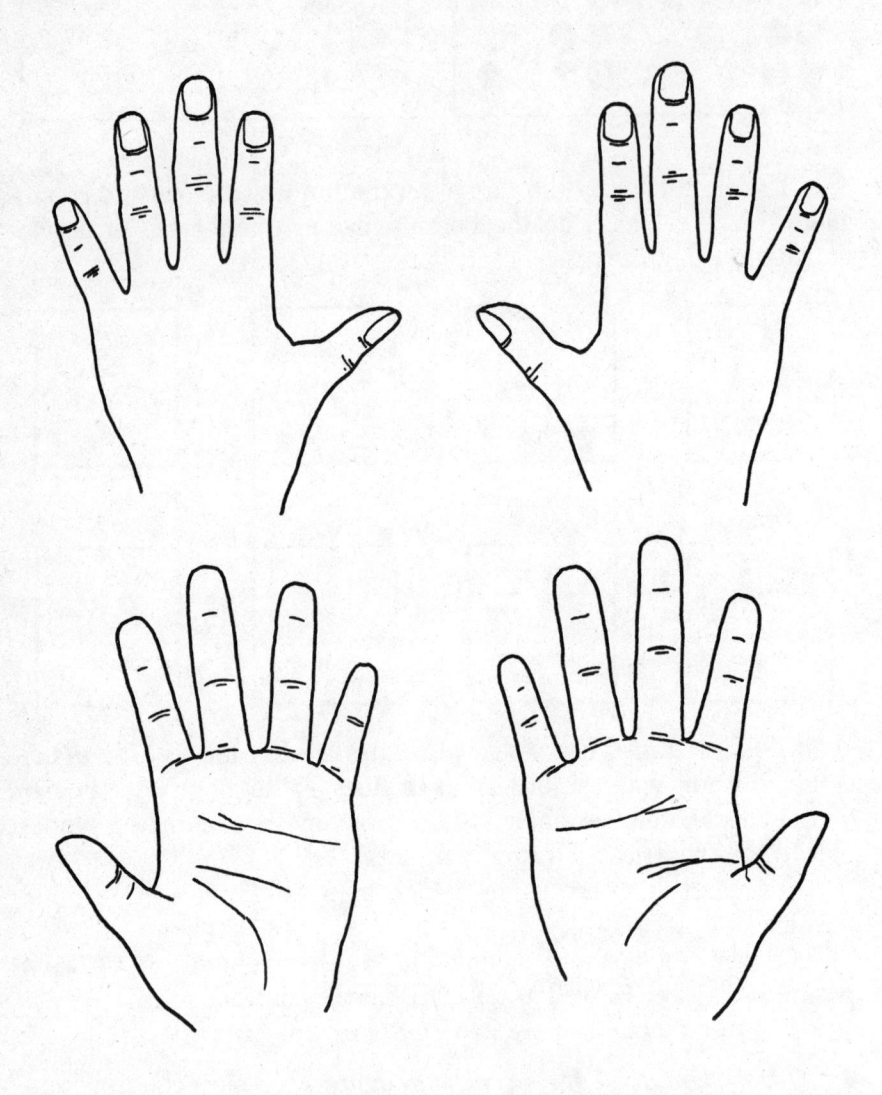

Teach children to adjust to the concept of right—left according to the direction faced. For example, show a picture looking at the back of a boy (later at the front). Which is his right hand? Which is his left leg?

Deficits in Body Awareness and Motor Control 117

Teach children directions.

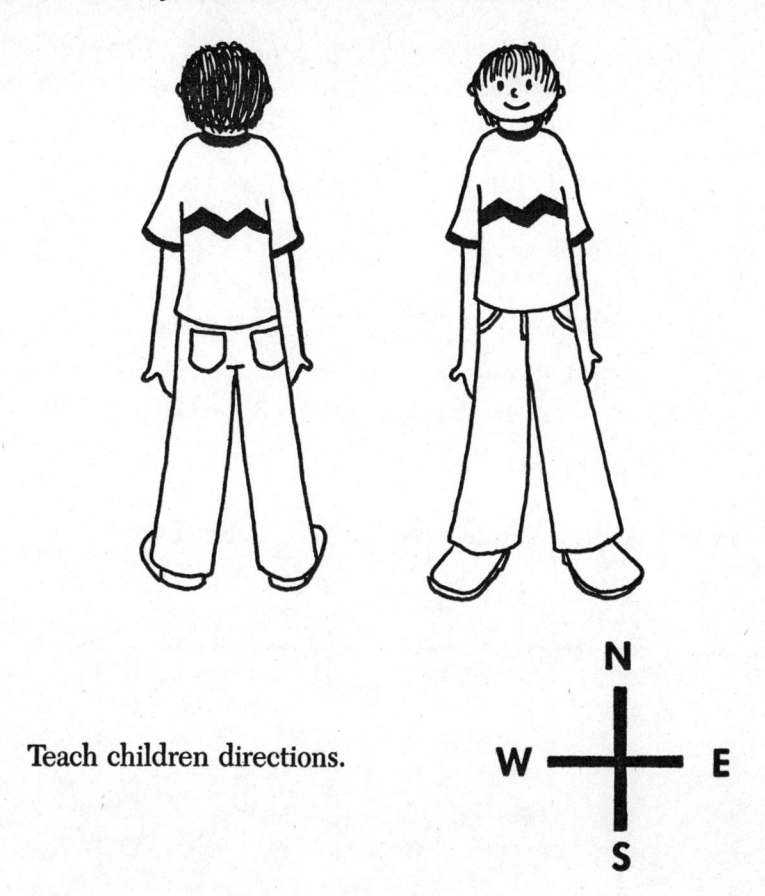

Children need experiences in identifying objects by feel. Put several objects in a bag: a spool, pen, small ball, pencil and a block. Ask the child to feel around until he finds the pencil, for example. Blindfold the child; put letters cut from sandpaper on a table. Ask the child to feel around until he locates a certain letter by feel.

DEVELOPING A PROGRAM FOR FINE MOTOR SKILLS

Handwriting is the first evidence of fine motor control. The child who has trouble with handwriting is easy to spot. In the average classroom there are usually 2-4 children who have severe enough problems in this area to warrant formation of a small group with the purpose of remediating these problems. Again a parent or aide can do the remediation if they understand the situation.

At the outset, the adult should realize there are multiple possible causes of the difficulty. It is necessary to carefully observe each child to determine the nature of the problem. Possible causes include:

1. poor instruction in handwriting.
2. left-handedness.
3. poor motor skills.
4. careless temperament.
5. faulty visual perception of letters and words.
6. an inability to retain visual impressions.
7. visual acuity problems.
8. disturbances in spatial perception.

It is easy to test handwriting. Give the child a pencil and a ditto such as the one shown here.

Task 1. Ask the child to trace along the dotted line. Caution him to do his very best to stay on the dots. Observe what he does. Watch his facial expression while working.

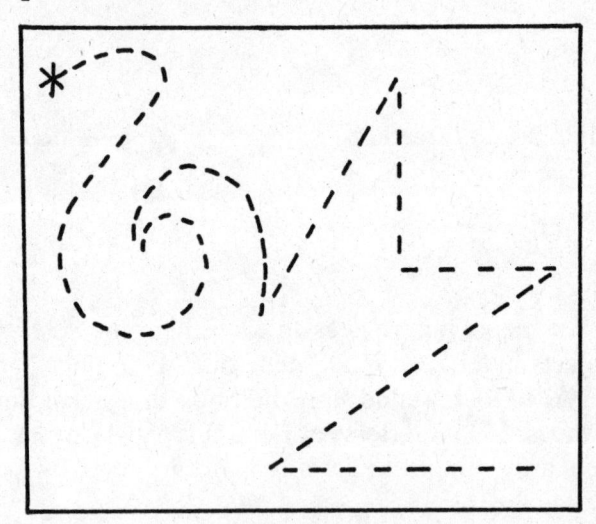

If the child does this task (staying *on* lines) without taking a long time or showing signs of effort (grunting, stopping, wanting to start over, tongue out) you know he has good motor control *and* he is not careless.

Task 2. Ask him to repeat the same exercise (use a new ditto). This time watch how he places his paper and holds his pencil, including which hand he is using and observe the way he holds his head and distance of his eyes from the paper. Look to see if there is

Deficits in Body Awareness and Motor Control

incorrect placement of the paper or faulty holding of a pencil because these can result in poor legibility. Also see if the child is favoring one eye over another by tilting his head/resting his head on the unused arm/getting very close or far from the writing surface. These behaviors mean that visual acuity should be checked by an opthalmologist.

Next, ask the child to trace the design on the ditto with the index finger of the hand he writes with, explaining as he goes how the design was made. You may need to help him. "It starts uphill, bends downhill and to the left side of the paper; moves upward and around to a point turning away and going uphill again, then curling downhill; going diagonally uphill; straight downhill, horizontally to the right, diagonally downhill and horizontally to the right." Have him retrace it with his finger. Make sure he is attentive.

Task 3. Now put the design away. Give him a blank sheet of paper and ask for him to reproduce the design from memory. If he can, you know he can accurately perceive the shape of letters and words and has no memory problems.

Task 4. Ask the child to carefully copy a short passage from his reading book. If the child is using adequate spacing/staying on the lines and not placing one letter on top of another he probably has no disturbances in his spatial perception.

In this test you are eliminating or locating causes. If the child performs all tasks accurately without evidence of eye problems, you are lucky. The child is only suffering from poor instruction in handwriting—a fairly simple matter to correct—but you or someone will have to take the time to retrace the skills he missed in previous instruction.

If during the test you located a cause for his dysagraphia (inability to write legibly) you will need to give remediating activities for that cause or for those causes, since some children have more than one problem. The suggestions that follow will help you:

The left-handed child—The child who has an established practice of writing with his left hand should be allowed to continue to do so. Placement of the paper should be as follows:

Manuscript Writing (Printed): The paper is placed directly in front of the child without a slant;

Cursive Writing: The top of the paper should be slanted north-northeast (just the opposite of the slant used by a righthanded person).

The pencil should be gripped just as a right-handed person would, only the left hand is used. Grip about 1 inch from the point with the end of the pencil directed toward the left shoulder. Many lefties want to curve the hand so it rests above where they are writing. Try to discourage this practice called hooking.

The child with poor motor skills—This child will need activities and supervision designed to develop his fine motor control. In the following activities be sure the paper is slanted properly and the pencil is held correctly.

Daily he should do some:

Coloring: Use big objects first (an apple for example). Teach child to outline, coloring toward center. Teach him to look at the shape of the object. If round, he should color with rounded motions. If square, he should color up and down or side to side. Concentrate on teaching him to stay within the lines.

Stencils and Dittoes: Clip the stencil to the paper so it cannot move. Have the child trace the form with the index finger of his writing hand. Then he will guide his pencil, trying to stay in the center of the roadway. The same sort of practice can be done with dittoes where the skill of drawing between the lines is taught. At first let him work with a dotted line to guide. Later present the same skill without dotted lines.

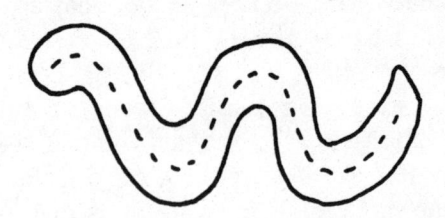

Once a child can control the movements of his pencil, a color-coded system may be used to teach the child how to form the letters.

Make color-coded sheets like the one shown on the next page, one for each child. (Since this book is printed in only black ink, the appropriate color is indicated next to each section of the letter. When making sheets for the children, use colored marking pens.)

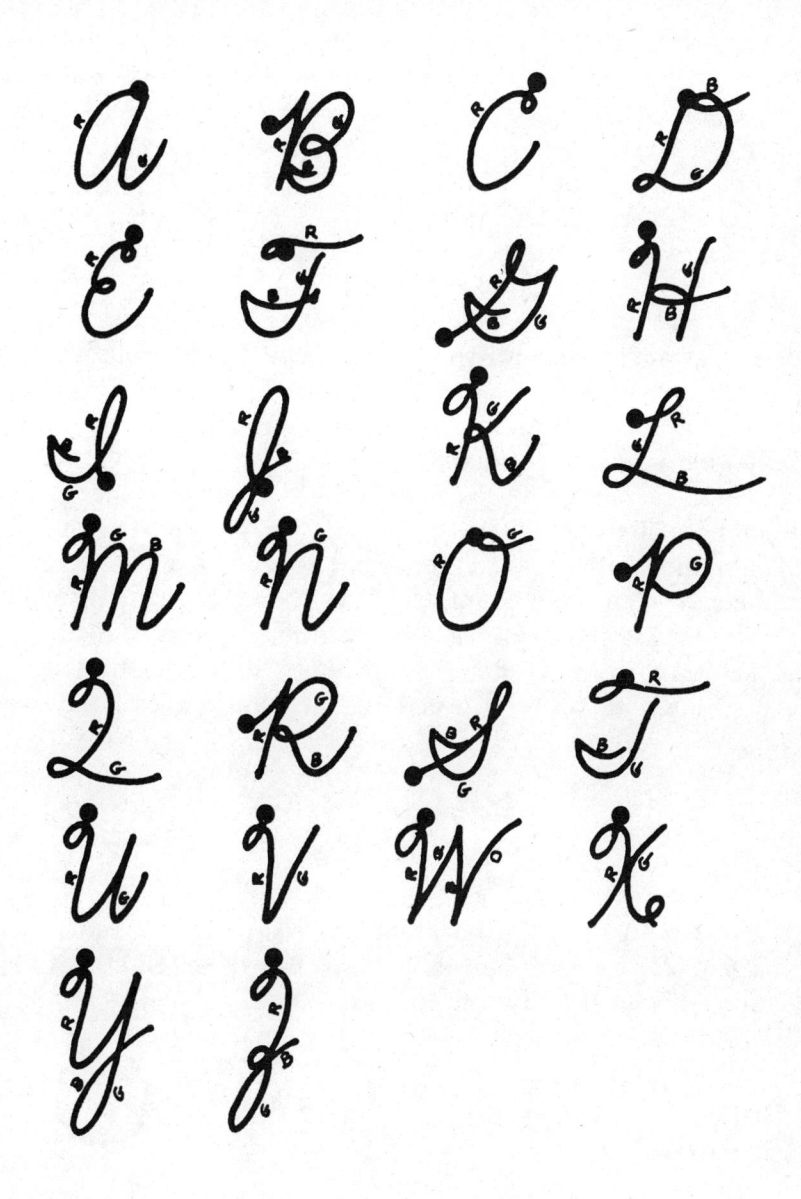

Deficits in Body Awareness and Motor Control 121

Begin at black dot •
Red (R) ⟶ Green (G) ⟶ Blue (B) ⟶ Orange (O)

The sample shown is designed to teach a child to form upper-case cursive letters. The same system can be used, however, for manuscript letters and for lower case. The child is taught to begin at black dot, move to red, then green then blue. If a fourth stroke is needed, add an orange line.

Paper-clip tracing paper on top of color-coded sheet. Ask child or children to place their pencil on the black dot of A. Say "we are going to make an A. Beginning on the black dot, move your pencil around the red line to the green line. What letter did we make?" (Children respond A)

You must guide the children's movements through each letter's colors and directions with your voice. Do not allow children to go ahead of your voice.

Follow this procedure daily—going through each letter separately—for 6 consecutive days.

On the seventh day, give the child the color-coded sheet to look at, but have him do each letter free hand. Do this three days in a row.

On the tenth day, ask the child to form a given letter, for example, a G, an S. Let them refer to color-coded sample if need be.

The final step is to ask the child to form all letters without visual support (from memory). Reteach any letters still giving trouble.

Gradually reduce the size of the letters until you reach this stage:

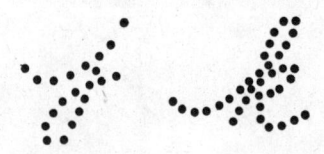

Work with the child on producing sharp corners and making circular motions. Teach him to feel how it is done. Guide his hand gently with your own if need be.

The careless child—To me this is the most difficult problem to solve. The child who doesn't care must be encouraged to slow down and may have to be motivated with some sort of rewards system.

The child with faulty perception of letters and words or the child with visual memory problems—This child needs dot-to-dot

Deficits in Body Awareness and Motor Control

practice. He needs to roll and form letters with clay ropes. He needs to feel sandpaper letters and stencils. Practice in forming letters with progressively reduced cues also helps:

k k l l l

The child with spatial perception problems—This child needs 1:1 supervision. He should have daily copying practice. At first give him a ditto with spaces to match whatever he is to copy.

<u>A</u> <u>b</u>a<u>t</u> <u>f</u>l<u>e</u>w <u>p</u>a<u>s</u>t <u>u</u><u>s</u>

Later the same exercise would be lined.

___ ___ ___ ___ ___

Finally, give the child lined paper. Sit by him reminding him to leave a space between each word while staying on the line.

In closing this chapter it seems appropriate to say a word about classroom management. If you operate on a 3 group system, it is simple to use movement activities as a group. A sample organization might be:

Group 1 (You)—Reading Instruction
Group 2 (Supervised by older child or parent)—Seatwork/Listening or Learning Centers
Group 3 (Supervised by parent aide)—Movement Activities

I strongly urge you to include a physical fitness program at all grade levels. In grades 4, 5 and 6, the Presidential Physical Fitness Program with its rewards is a great motivator.

8

How to Help Children Who Demonstrate Problems in Language Development And Conceptual Thinking

If I were asked what is the most common learning disability, I would cite a lack of language development. When the average child enters school, he speaks in sentences and is able to process information delivered to him in short sentences. A large percentage of learning disabled children cannot do these things. Therefore, essential to improving this child's academic performance is engaging him in a planned program that will teach him names for common objects, how to form sentences, and meanings for words which involve conceptual thinking. The program must also provide for feedback, so the child demonstrates he understands what is said to him and that he can also use language sufficiently well to communicate his thoughts to others. Unfortunately the child who has problems in the areas of language and conceptual thinking does not outgrow them. He can, however, make great progress if his teacher concentrates on remediating in these areas.

RECOGNIZING A CHILD WITH PROBLEMS WITH LANGUAGE AND CONCEPTUAL THINKING

Spotting this child early is simple. He points and says "I want that" because he lacks the vocabulary to name the object. He cannot follow oral directions—indeed he may appear not even to have heard them. When asked a short question he answers in incomplete sentences but if asked a long sentence (more than 5 words) he may say

Language Development

"What?" If this child is not provided with a strong language development program in the primary grades, he may reach the fourth grade able to read words but with no idea of what they mean. He also will be unable to perform adequately in any subject matter area, since he is unable to comprehend what the text tells him.

The older the child gets before being involved in a language development program, the greater will be his problem. Language is like an inverted pyramid—if concepts or vocabulary are missing, the whole structure is likely to fall in a shamble. As an adult this person may suffer socially because he cannot read the emotions of others, cannot predict the outcome in a social situation, and feels isolated because he cannot adequately communicate with others. I urge you—regardless of grade level taught—to include in your daily program activities like the ones which follow.

CLASS DISCUSSION FOR LANGUAGE DEVELOPMENT

One day in our reading we came across the concept of *waiting room* as we read about a little boy's trip to the dentist. The children I taught at the time were 7 years old, had lived in a rural parish of Louisiana all their lives, and with only one exception none of them had ever been in or heard of a waiting room. We looked at the picture in the book and the conversation went like this:

Teacher: "How many of you have been in a waiting room?"
David: "I have."
Teacher: "Where?"
David: "I cut my foot open. It had to be sewed up."
(*Note:* He answered *why* not where which alerted me that he didn't under the concept *where*).
Teacher: "David, I'm glad you've been to a waiting room so you can tell the other children more about it. I asked *where*, you told me why. Where was it? A doctors office? a hospital?"

David nodded when I said "hospital." I asked if any of the other children had been to a hospital. No one had, so David and I had to explain what a hospital was. (Several weeks later we did a week's unit on nurses, hospitals, doctors, and medical instruments).

We talked about a waiting room, looking at the picture, and the children came up with a definition, "A waiting room is a place where people can wait."

Teacher: "Could people be waiting in a waiting room for a plane?"

The children decided they could *if* there were chairs.
Teacher: "Could people wait for a bus?"

Later in the week, we took a field trip to the city, visiting the airport waiting room and a clinic waiting room. We expanded the concept to include a theater "lobby" where people stand to wait and a church "foyer" where people wait.

Pictures in texts or movies are a natural place to begin a conversation. In a social studies book, a picture of a harvesting machine can become a fly-off point for discussing and collecting pictures of tools/machines. Ask "What is a machine? Is it a thing that has wheels?" If the children say "yes," show them a picture of a washer. "Does this have wheels? It is a machine." Keep plugging until the children eliminate all the trivia and end up with the essence of the word machine. "It is a device to help us do work more easily."

In explaining a concept like machines, it is essential to provide many samples for examination so maximum learning occurs.

If pictures aren't available, try talking activities such as the following which occurred with the word "amaze."

Teacher: "What does "amaze" mean?
No response.
Teacher: "Have you heard this word before?"
Children thought they had but could not recall context in which it was used.
Teacher: "Let me give you some sample sentences and you see if you can figure out what amaze means."
"A little girl stood on her hands with her feet in the air for 5 minutes. I was amazed she could do that."
"A wheel fell off the car as the car passed me. I am amazed the car did not get wrecked."
"I was amazed because the boy ate six hamburgers."

Keep on until someone is able to say "amaze" means about the same as "surprised." Be sure to compliment this child—perhaps reward him with a sticker (young kids love those good work stickers that smell like grapes or bananas). Praising and rewarding serve to motivate the other children to listen, think and be involved in this detective-like process of finding a word's meaning. Once the meaning is located, repeat it. Use the same sentences you gave as clues but instead of saying amazed say "surprised."

Language Development

The next step is to ask each child to make a complete sentence of their own using "amaze." Ask them to relate to "What would amaze you?"

In my group one child said—and everyone laughed— "I'd be amazed if my little brother treated me nice."

Since language development, perceptual awareness and thinking are experience related, they can obviously be improved by what we as teachers do. Prior to receiving your new class of students in September, survey each textbook you are required to use and make a list of words (at your grade level) which you will use in a language development program. Choose a variety.

Words that convey a concept—such as beauty, trade, climate, plateau—and words which convey values—such as truth, courage, beauty—should be developed so the child may use them in his daily vocabulary and thinking.

ACTIVITIES FOR PERCEPTION, CONCEPTUAL THINKING AND LANGUAGE DEVELOPMENT

On the pages that follow, you will find suggested activities that will serve to

1. Enhance perception,
2. Develop conceptual thinking, and
3. Help in developing language.

If you used one activity per day, this list would last until approximately the middle of the school year. By that point, your students will be suggesting ideas and you will think of others.

Activity 1

- Bring in 2 or 3 vegetables, for example, an onion, a pepper and a string bean.
- Cut them in half. Look at the cross section.
- Discuss likenesses, differences, size, color, shape.

Activity 2

- Give each child a piece of yarn 18 inches long;
- Ask them to paste it, without cutting, into some sort of design;
- Talk about several samples.

Activity 3

- Give each child a circle, square, triangle, rectangle—vary size and color;
- Ask them to paste them into a design;
- Talk about 3 or 4 samples.

Activity 4

- Ask children to collect and bring in bird feathers;
- Talk about size, shape, color, feel.

Activity 5

- Have scraps of fabric (prints as well as solid colors), yarn, ribbon, buttons;
- Ask children to select 4 to go together;
- Discuss why they chose as they did.

Activity 6

- Ask children to bring in empty cereal boxes;
- Talk about designs;
- Take a note on which one has the most *appealing* design. (Explain the meaning of appeal.)

Activity 7

- Bring in a bag of unshelled peanuts. Give 3-5 to each child.
- Look at the different shapes;
- Each child guesses how many nuts are in one of his five;
- Open them; see if the guess was right. Eat the lesson.

Activity 8

- Give each child 3 pipe cleaners and 2 minutes to bend them into a design;
- Discuss shapes made.

Activity 9

- Ask each child to choose a crayon of his favorite color from a big box of broken assorted crayons;
- Make a tally of what they chose to determine which crayon was first, second, third in popularity;

Language Development

- Think and share how children feel about color. "What color is happy?" "Is there a sad color?" "A warm one?" "A cold one?"
- Make a bar graph of their tally. Look at at least 2 other bar graphs.

Activity 10

- Ask each child to bring in one "container." (Explain that a container is a jar, box, bottle, basket, package).
- Talk about what could be put in each. Teach concept of size, shape.

Activity 11

- Bring in a bell, a whistle and a long piece of paper.
- Children close their eyes. Teacher makes a noise with each.
- Children identify sound.
- Close eyes. Listen for all the sounds they can hear in the room. While eyes are closed, teacher makes 3 sounds: door closing, chalk writing, ticking.
- Talk about how noises are made. "What noises are pleasant?" "What noises are unpleasant and why?"

Activity 12

- Bring in a bag of objects, for example, a spool, a button, a ball of yarn, scissors, a cookie, a pencil, a piece of cotton.
- Without looking, let the children identify and keep an object if they guess right by feel.
- Talk about how things feel. Develop knowledge of adjectives.

Activity 13

- Put a piece of sponge, a piece of sandpaper, a piece of burlap and a piece of velvet on a card (one for each child).
- Wet sponge.
- Talk about how they feel. Develop new vocabulary soft, moist, coarse, smooth.

Activity 14

- Give each child a frame. (Cut a piece of black construction paper so you have a hole in center.)
- Ask them to look for good pictures out of doors, as you would

when focusing a camera. The construction paper acts as a picture frame. Talk about what they see and like.

Activity 15

- Together collect leaves from different types of trees. Look at the trees for foliage patterns.
- Look at them with a magnifying glass.
- Discuss color, shape, size; talk about differences.
- Place leaf under a sheet of paper; color over it by turning crayon on its side.
- Use white glue, around each outline. Let it dry; feel outline or shape of each leaf.

Activity 16

- In autumn, collect and look at all the different colors of a leaf.
- Give ditto with 4 leaves (same type). Color them orange-red, brown.
- Discuss the seasons Talk about clothing appropriate to seasons. Learn to name the seasons in order.

Activity 17

- Bring in an apple, orange.
- Cut in half (cross-section).
- Put tempera paint on each cross section. Print onto paper.
- Talk about designs, lines.

Activity 18

- Talk about a continuous line. The pencil never comes off the page.
- Draw a sample:

- Let them draw and discuss what they did.

Language Development

Activity 19

- Take a walking trip near school. Look at trees. Check growth patterns, various barks, and color-shape of leaves. Talk about textures, etc. Renew rough, coarse, smooth.

Activity 20

- Ask each child to bring a piece of jewlery.
- Compare, discuss.
- Identify stones: pearl, jade, turquoise.

Activity 21

- Bring 3 items, example, a can, a coin, a paper clip.
- Blindfold someone. Ask him to identify things by feel and tell how they knew.

Activity 22

- Discuss shapes.
- Let children use stencils to make letters of their name. Show them how to center on lines;
- Learn "stencil" and the word "pattern."

Activity 23

- Collect soft things—cotton, fur, foam (sponge), feathers. Get children to talk about other things that are hard/soft.

Activity 24

- Look at clouds on a cloudy day.
- Discuss color, shape, size.
- Try to imagine a pattern in certain clouds—see a picture in the cloud. Discuss what you see. Extend concept of pattern.

Activity 25

- Look at 3 kinds of house plants.
- Discuss likenesses and differences.

Activity 26

- Bring in a collection of things to feel: bread dough, corduroy, sand, hair, silk, their own skin.
- Compare and discuss.

Activity 27

- Bring in several kinds of nuts (in shells);
- Compare and discuss likenesses and differences.

Activity 28

- Have children place whole hand on paper, fingers outstretched, and draw around it.
- Looking, they fill in some details such as nails, joint lines.
- Talk about how you'd draw an arm. What details would they include? Words—joint, wrist, elbow.

Activity 29

- Collect several apples: red, golden, green;
- What is the essence of an apple.
- Taste them. Discuss differences in *flavor*, juiciness. Learn words such as tart, sweet.

Activity 30

- Talk about ghosts, fairies, leprauchauns.
- Ask each child to tell a trick he'd play if he were one of these imaginary creatures. Build complete sentences.

Activity 31

- Obtain a copy of Walt Disney's record *Chilling, Thrilling Sounds of the Haunted House* from public library or elsewhere.
- Play and discuss.
- Which sound is the scariest?

Activity 32

- Be alert any time you show a movie with sound; re-run the movie without turning on the projection bulb. Let the children listen to the sound track. Identify the sound. Confirm the guess by re-running it with the bulb on.

Language Development

Activity 33

- Wet white paper.
- Using water paint, put dabs of color on and watch it spread.
- When dry, add designs/lines in between with black felt tip markers.
- Share and talk about results.

Activity 34

- Bring in fish pictures. (Most bookstores have fish/bird/animal stamp books.)
- Compare and discuss size, shape, color.

Activity 35

- Bring in bottles of soap bubbles.
- With wand, make bubbles.
- Look for colors. Talk about the colors in light.

Activity 36

- Bring in collection of sea shells.
- Talk about them (homes).
- Sketch a few.

Activity 37

- Ask children to bring in a favorite picture from a magazine or a snapshot.
- Have them share why they especially like it.

Activity 38

- Bring in a set of spices and flavorings, for example, ground cloves, mint extract, vanilla extract, bay leaves.
- Have child close his eyes and smell. Try to guess color by smell.
- Try to develop awareness so each child can identify spice by its smell.

Activity 39

- Bring in 3 boxes: a tiny, a medium size, and a large one.
- Discuss what could be put in each.
- Personalize it. Ask them to pretend it's a birthday gift. "What's in the box?"

Activity 40

- Bring in some kitchen tools.
- Look at them. What are they for?
- Extend vocabulary.

Activity 41

- Bring in some garage tools.
- Look at them. What are they used for?
- What are their names?

Activity 42

- Find 6 glasses of the same shape, size.
- Fill them with varying amounts of water.
- Tap the rim with a spoon.
- Develop songs to go with different tones.
- Talk about high pitch, low pitch.

Activity 43

- Make a homemade guitar from a cigar box. Place thumb tacks across opening and stretch rubber bands of various sizes or widths.
- Pluck it to hear different sounds.
- Reinforce concept of high pitch vs. low pitch.

Activity 44

- Discuss skeletons.
- Take a walking trip to look at trees, now without leaves.
- Sketch what they saw: trees with thick trunks, others with spindly trunks.
- Develop vocabulary: spindly, thick, skeleton.

Activity 45

- Bring in foods: salty crackers, avocado, fruit roll.
- Taste and compare with words like salty, crunchy, bland, tart.

Activity 46

- Listen for sounds in room with eyes closed.

Language Development

- You can add some such as fingers tapping, chalk writing.
- Discuss where they came from and what made them.

Activity 47

- Go outdoors. With eyes closed listen for sounds.
- Identify sounds.

Activity 48

- Talk about Indian names such as Running Deer, Clearwater, Big Bear.
- Ask each child to think for 3 minutes. Choose and discuss the Indian name they would like.

Activity 49

- Obtain a book about Indian masks.
- Talk about the Indians use of bright colors.
- Ask children where the Indians got paint from.
- Introduce concept of vivid color.

Activity 50

- Develop vocabulary words *straight* and *curved* surface.
- Draw curved and straight lines.
- Look around the room. Identify objects that have curved surfaces and objects with straight surfaces.

Activity 51

- Gather pictures from sports articles, newspaper.
- Talk about "action."
- Play Statues game. Children move freely, freeze on signal. Have them observe positions they freeze in.
- Develop concept of position.

Activity 52

- Talk about *overlapping*—creating the 2-dimensional (illusion of space).
- Arrange vegetables or fruit overlapping.
- Sketch what they see (remind them to study "contour" of each item), or you may have shapes precut so they can paste them, overlapping them.

Activity 53

- Talk about concept of *value*—essence is that a thing need not be expensive to have value. It must only be meaningful to a person.
- Tell them their home is rapidly burning. They can only save 2 things. Give 3 minutes thinking time. What would they take out and why?
- Discuss answers.

Activity 54

- Look at a collection of animal pictures.
- Talk about shape, form and feel of animals.
- Draw stick pictures to represent. Use Ed Emberley's book to extend activity for several days.[10]

Activity 55

- Use modeling clay.
- Make balls, strings of various sizes, thicknesses.
- Using various tools—straw, toothpick, popsicle stick, key, coin—make impressions and discuss.

Activity 56

- Use a piano to demonstrate different tones.
- Teach simple 1 note at a time songs (you don't have to be a pianist to do this). These can be Christmas tunes.

Activity 57

- Get a set of bells.
- Talk about which bell is loudest, which makes high tone/low tone. The bells can combine with Christmas theme nicely.
- Develop the meaning of the word tone.

Activity 58

- Develop concepts of opaque/translucent.
- Using colored tissue paper (lets light through) and 2 pieces of black construction paper they can create a neat picture.

---

[10] Ed Emberley, *Drawing Book of Animals* (Boston, 1970: Little, Brown & Co.)

Language Development

- Cut design in construction paper holding 2 pieces together so the pattern is the same.
- Place tissue paper between the sheets of construction paper. Staple and glue. The Christmas Tree or bell of tissue paper are attractive.

Activity 59

- Cut strings of heavy cord.
- Dip them in plaster of paris (work quickly before it hardens).
- Allow children to shape strings into ornaments (let them dry on wax paper).
- Teach meaning of word ornament.

Activity 60

- Collect pictures of animals of prey. Develop concept of prey.
- If possible go to a museum/zoo where these animals can be viewed.
- Discuss what makes the animal able to catch other animals.

Activity 61

- Reinforce concept of curved.
- With clay, design a curved sculpture.
- Talk about samples.

Activity 62

- Ask children to name a favorite food.
- Describe it by color, taste, texture, smell.
- Bring a sample of it in and have a "tasting day."

Activity 63

- Plan a finger painting activity using tempera mixed with starch (half and half).
- Explore and discuss the different effects:
  zig zags   wide lines
  wiggles   narrow lines
  curves   straight lines
  fingertip dots

Activity 64

- Look at pictures of several birds.
- Discuss color, size, shape differences.
- Ask them to pretend they are petting a bird. They feel over round head, down neck curve, up the tail feathers, under belly sloop and up and over the bill. Introduce word "contour."
- Ask volunteers to come to the board and with chalk, go through the motions.
- Discuss. Reinforce contour by having them feel lumps and bumps "contour" of their face.

Activity 65

- Listen to music for different moods.
- Encourage them to direct tempo with hands as the orchestra leader does.
- Talk about flow, speed, intensity.

Activity 66

- Bring in a piece of paper for each four children.
- Establish order in which paper will pass.
- Let each child draw on the paper for 15 seconds, then pass it on.
- Discuss results.
- Display results. Repeat activity 3 days in a row.

Activity 67

- Talk about fingerprints.
- Using an ink pad, explore clenched fist, finger print patterns.

Language Development

- Talk about fingerprints being used in finding criminals.

Activity 68

- Set out 5 or 6 sound makers, example, a coin, a bottle with a top which makes noise as it unscrews, a glass of water with a pan to pour into, a sheet of paper to rattle, a book to slam shut.
- Blindfold someone.
- Let them identify each sound as to source.
- Let someone else identify direction from which sound comes.

Activity 69

- Place sounds on tape: typewriter, dog bark, leafing through pages of a book, snoring, whistling.
- Ask children to identify sounds.

Activity 70

- Place water in small jars: cool, warm, cold.
- Children will identify which is which.
- Extend activity by asking children to respond appropriately:

  Tea should be served _____.
  Baths are nicer when they are _____.
  Winters normally are _____.

Activity 71

- Talk about opposites.
- Demonstrate
    open a book—close a book
    open a door—close a door
    move fast—move slow
    go in—go out
- Together develop a list of opposites.
- Hang it up; add to it in coming days.

Activity 72

- Obtain some grass seed and blotter paper.
- Wet blotter paper; let grass seed germinate between 2 pieces.
- Teach meaning of "sprout" and relate it to children sprouting or growing.

Activity 73

- Gather several kinds of weeds, wild plants, grass.
- Look at them with magnifying glass.
- Discuss veins, extend vocabulary to looking at human veins.

Activity 74

- Talk about molds/frames/forms.
- Use plaster of paris molds to extend concept.
- If possible visit a construction site to see forms.

Activity 75

- Bring in pictures of different kinds of butterflies. (These can be purchased in booklet form at most bookstores.)
- Discuss colors, different shapes.

Activity 76

- Look at several different types of flowers.
- Discuss likeness/difference.

Activity 77

- Note that a single word can have many different meanings.
- Stimulate interest by developing posters regarding a few of those words. The following will give you some ideas for the kinds of words to choose:

"Note" for example, can be a written message, a musical symbol, paying attention to detail.

A whole lesson can be developed around note. Help the children write a *thank you* note. Teach them to draw a music note and show them how to read musical notes. Ask and help them make sentences using "note."

Bolt is another word with multiple meanings: a bolt of cloth, a bolt of lightning, bolt across the room, a nut and bolt, bolt the door.

Fire presents opportunities: build a fire, fire a gun, fire an employee.

It is important to develop a child's ability to recognize the meaning of *gestures* (develop the concept). By miming demostrate:

Language Development

"I don't know"—shrug.
"Its okay"—form an "o" with fingers.
"Come here"—wiggling finger toward you.

A colleague had a system she used which seemed a good idea to me. She had a *Word for a Day* "show" each morning. Her aide came on the show with a name such as *Nonsense*. She interviewed Nonsense, who in turn demonstrated samples of nonsense. At the end of The Show the class came up with a meaning for the word. If a student was able to appropriately use *nonsense* in his work that day, he was rewarded.

Special holidays such as Halloween, Thanksgiving, Christmas, Valentines Day, Easter provide us with great opportunities to enhance vocabulary, e.g., "Tis the *season* to be *jolly*" with lessons on hanging *boughs of holly* and listening to the beautiful holiday music which ranges from happy sleigh bell songs to serious religious songs. By relating history and showing pictures we can develop a child's appreciation of how the holiday can be celebrated differently as in Scrooge's case. The sounds and foods of a holiday extend perception.

In summary, our teaching in the language development area is a matter of how alert we are to words. We can vary our daily vocabulary to increase the child's awareness.

"Get your book and turn to page __" can become, "Obtain a book and turn to page __." On another day you can say "Avail yourself of a book and open it to page __."

Imagination allows us limitless possibilities for development. As you think about it, you will come up with other activities to add to the list in this chapter.

A final problem exists in the area of language development. Occasionally you will find a child who has a problem saying a word. Chimney is a commonly mispronounced word that comes out "chim-i-ney." There are others, of course, but the rule for remediation is this:

1. Visually show the child how many syllables the word contains:
    Chim (1)   ney (2)
2. Have him put up 2 fingers.
3. He says *chim..chim..chim* on finger 1.
4. He says *ney..ney..ney* on finger 2.
5. Then you ask him to be certain to say the syllables together—one syllable for each finger—allowing no other noises to creep in. If he can do it, great! If not, repeat steps 1-4 and on step 5

have him say it with you watching your mouth. Say it with a long pause:

Between syllables *chim*. . . . .*ney*.
Repeat.
Repeat.
Repeat, gradually shortening the gap between the syllables.

As I close this chapter I'd like to relate a story from personal experience. I firmly believe, from this experience, that a strong language development program can improve intelligence scores. A few years ago, I worked in a special project in rural Louisiana called Readiness. At that time children were entering grade 1 without the benefit of a pre-school or kindergarten program. Some children were not "ready" for first grade work. I was asked to select these children, teach them for one year in a readiness situation and prepare them for first grade. I went into the first-grade classrooms, observed and selected 15 children who seemed to be functioning below the average level. We had these children tested at the nearest university. Of the 15 children, 14 received IQ scores between 65 and 75 and were therefore considered mildly retarded. The 15th child scored a 90. For the next year, I bombarded the children with activities to increase their perceptual and language abilities. In May, these children were retested at the university. On the repeat testing only 5 children received scores below 75. Nine children demonstrated a rise in IQ from the 65-75 range to the 85-95 range, and the 15th child who previously scored 90 showed a rise to 115. These results were sufficient to convince me of the value of a strong language emphasis. I did not remain in Louisiana to watch these children perform the next year in regular first grade. I cannot help but believe they did better than they would have without the readiness experience.

Based on this experience, I feel the importance of providing such a program and devoting time for adequate feedback so you know the children are incorporating what they've learned into their daily lives.

9

How to Help Children Who Demonstrate Problems In Attention or Behavior

In the average class there are usually several children who have problems in the area of attention. They may be hyperactive, hypoactive, epileptic or show signs of emotional disturbance. This chapter will suggest some specific ways you can help these children.

HOW TO RECOGNIZE CHILDREN WHO ARE HYPERACTIVE, HYPOACTIVE OR EPILEPTIC

Read the following vignettes and you'll probably substitute names of students you've known for the names used here.

George might be described as a "human yo-yo." He is up, down, lies under his desk, talks incessantly, drums his fingers, fidgets. He is hyperactive, and you feel exhausted from just watching him. He cannot get his assignments completed because so much of his time is being used up by nontask-related behaviors. What he does accomplish is sloppily and carelessly done. George may also do things which make him appear emotionally disturbed such as yelling out in class, being aggressive, bothering others and even destroying the property of others.

Karen, on the other hand, is listless; sometimes she falls asleep. Her responses are slow. She prefers to sit at recess. Her work is not completed either. She can be described as being hypoactive.

Morgan is an epileptic. He has not had a seizure at school but he has them occasionally at home. Each of these children can be helped. Each of these children needs to be under medical supervision. If they are not, they should be referred to a qualified pediatric neurologist. A referral letter should be given to the parent to take to the doctor; that letter should request that the doctor make a written report to the school if the child's condition has academic implications.

Help for the Hyperactive Child

In the case of the child who is hyperactive, the physician may conduct an encephalographic (EEG) examination. What does an EEG show? It will determine if the child has specific neurological damage or a seizure (epileptic) pattern. Epilepsy patterns are found in some LD children. If so, the child may need anti-convulsant medication even though he has not had a seizure. The EEG may also reveal a lesion in a particular brain hemisphere. (Recent research indicates lesions in the left cerebral hemisphere affect the child's ability to acquire and use language, while lesions in the right cerebral hemisphere may impair the child's spatial skills/motor or manipulatory skills. Frontal lobe damage may result in impulsive hyperactive behavior or inability of the child to think abstractly.)[11] This information is helpful in developing a teacher's patience in working with a learning-disabled child. As teachers we must guard against the tendency to say that a child is just "not trying." His poor performance may not result from lack of effort—there may be a physiological basis for his slow progress. Finally, the doctor may recommend Ritalin drug therapy if the EEG rules out the possibility of seizure discharges. Ritalin (the preferred drug for hyperactivity) has the effect of increasing attention span, alleviating some visual-perceptual confusion, decreasing impulsivity, and calming the child. The teacher should carefully observe and report to the physician whether the Ritalin is accomplishing its desired effect. If it is not, the physician may change the dosage (children vary in the amount needed) or may switch to a different medication all together. Ritalin is contraindicated if it causes insomnia, loss of appetite, headache, stomach ache, depression, irritability, or skin rash.

The use of Ritalin and other stimulants in the treatment of hyperactivity has been the subject of much controversy. As an educator, I can attest to its value in calming children and rendering

---

[11]A more comprehensive explanation of brain function is given by Tanis Bryan and James Bryan in *Understanding Learning Disabilities* (Port Washington, N.Y.: Alfred Publishing Co., 1975), pp. 70-88.

them able to achieve. George's behavior, for example, made a dramatic, and instant change under the drug's influence. So much so, that I could look at him as he walked into the classroom first thing in the morning and know immediately if his mother had given him his pill. If she had not, it was pointless to work with him. The school nurse would verify with the mother that he had not had it, give him one (we had a bottle at school) and in 45 minutes return him to class for instruction. George was a nonreader until he began taking medication—then he began to make terrific strides. In deciding whether a child should be medicated, a physician must weigh the possible and yet unknown damage a drug can do against the almost certain fact that the truly hyperactive child will not learn without it.

A second possible cause of hyperactivity is diet. Dr. Benjamin Feingold in his book *Why Your Child Is Hyperactive* suggests that modern food-preservatives, colorings and flavorings may cause hyperactivity. Again, the evidence is not all in, but from my experience, it appears to me that diet does play a part.

The Hypoactive Child

In the case of Karen, we found her hypoactivity was probably due to an extreme case of anemia. It is hard to believe that in a land of plenty a child could be malnourished. However, in Karen's case it was true. She ate poorly and not because her parents were poor. A balanced diet was offered at home but Karen "didn't like" most foods. She perked up considerably after vitamin therapy was begun. The number of conditions that can cause hypoactivity are too numerous to explore here. It is only necessary that we, as teachers, realize that a healthy child has the energy to play and work. Hypoactivity indicates a mental or physical problem that necessitates medical intervention.

The Epileptic Child

As for Morgan, the epileptic child, the teacher needs to know that an attack of epilepsy occurs when there is a burst of electrical energy in the brain. The seizure may take three forms:

    a. Grand mal—the victim losses consciousness, falls if not supported, muscles jerk. The duration varies from several seconds to a few minutes.

    b. Petit mal—the victim loses awareness of his surroundings for a few seconds. He does not lose consciousness.

c. Psychomotor—the victim acts withdrawn or behaves oddly for a period of a few seconds or minutes; may rock in seat, dig at clothing, roam about room in a dazed state.

Refer a potentially epileptic child to a physician. Modern anticonvulsant drug therapy is very effective.

If a teacher has been alerted that she has an epileptic child in her class, it is wise to prepare the class for the possibility of that child having a seizure. A grand mal seizure is a frightening thing to witness. A little knowledge on the part of the children will reduce the trauma to the other children. No matter how much the child knows, his first experience with an epileptic will shock him, but knowing what to expect may prevent pandemonium in the classroom. Certainly, if a teacher must take care of the epileptic child, she cannot handle the pandemonium also. I suggest doing the following:

- Talk with the child and his parents about the need for telling the other children (so the teacher can devote her whole attention to their child during the seizure).
- When the teacher explains it to the class she should (a) treat it as unemotionally as she would if she were explaining why she wears glasses— "It's a medical problem," (b) prepare the children for what they will see, and (c) enlist the class' help in watching out for the epileptic child, particularly if the seizure occurs on the playground and she is not present.

The children should know that you *never put anything in an epileptic's mouth*—not a hankerchief (which can be choked on) nor a pencil or spoon (which can cause injury). Children should be instructed to leave the convulsing child alone for he will soon come out of the seizure; they can help by removing things that are hot or sharp from his reach and going for help (principal/nurse/teacher). The children must not tease or embarrass the child who has had a seizure. Following a seizure the epileptic child needs complete rest. He may sleep deeply for hours.

Perseveration

A final phenomenon needing mention is perseveration. A few examples of this behavior are the child who claps or laughs or counts long after the rest of the children have stopped or the child who continues on and on an incorrect response after you have indicated its

Problems of Attention of Behavior

inappropriateness. A firm hand on the shoulder, eye contact and an emphatic "No!" will generally end perseveration.

HOW TO RECOGNIZE AND HELP CHILDREN WHO SHOW DIFFICULTIES IN EMOTIONAL ADJUSTMENT

A child may experience severe problems of adjustment, such as:

1. Aggression (bullying, constantly fighting).
2. Withdrawal (loner).
3. Cruelty to others (people/animals).
4. Extreme destructiveness.
5. Lying/stealing regularly, particularly if the lying is counterproductive (as in cases where the truth would be more acceptable than an obvious lie)
6. Impulsivity that is frequent and angers others (child who in a tantrum throws books, desk, pencil).

The child needs competent guidance and counselling. The school should refer the parents and child to a guidance agency such as Family Service Assn. of America. Other competent child guidance agencies will be known to your local Juvenile Probation Department; generally probation officers can give you names of competent agencies and are glad to assist you in this way.

While the child is in therapy—often an extended process involving months—the teacher must have some techniques for dealing with these kinds of behaviors. Refer to Chapter 2 for general suggestions as to prevention, use of reward and aversive techniques. There are specific cautions to use when working with disturbed children.

The most important is, *do not show favoritism to the disturbed child*. *Unacceptable behavior* (lying, stealing, bullying, tantrums and other impulsive acts) *is contagious*. If you allow such behavior to go unpunished, you will lose control of the rest of your class. If such behaviors occur, *punishment will be most effective if it is immediate*.

Talk with your principal at the beginning of the year and come to some joint agreement as to how you will handle situations of this sort. If this sort of situation occurs at a time near recess or during a time when you can leave your group to deal with the situation, there is no problem. Follow the discipline suggestions at the end of Chapter 2. However, if the infraction occurs at a time when you cannot deal immediately with it, I feel the child should be removed from the group until you can. If your school has a child guidance teacher/principal/nurse perhaps that person can supervise the child until you can see him alone.

Time out may work. Enlisting the cooperation of a fellow teacher is another possibility. For example the sixth grade teacher in my school sometimes would send a disturbing youngster with an assignment to my second grade room. Likewise my second graders were very intimidated by being sent to sit in a sixth grade room. Merely removing the child from your room serves as a warning to other children that they must conduct themselves in acceptable ways at all times.

Above all, do not allow one child to disrupt the educational process in your room.

Section 3

SKILLS DEVELOPMENT IN GIVEN SUBJECT AREAS

10

How to Teach Remedial Reading

About one child of every seven will experience difficulty learning to read and will need remedial instruction.

The program outlined in this chapter has the following advantages:

1. The child has not been previously exposed to it.
2. It is designed to produce results in a short time,
3. It is simple for a teacher to follow.
4. The approach involves using all the child's modalities: visual, auditory, tactile.
5. The teaching of spelling is incorporated.
6. It requires no expenditures of money for the purchase of workbooks or texts.

This program was not designed for the child who has never been exposed to reading. It is designed for the child who has failed with the traditional approaches and needs an approach that looks different.

VISUAL SUPPORTS FOR TEACHING READING

1. Make a permanent bulletin board of colorful short vowel cards. Use 8" x 11" plain white paper, color one design on each card with felt pens. Display in an area permanently, near where students will do reading. Build the habit in students of referring to the bulletin board.

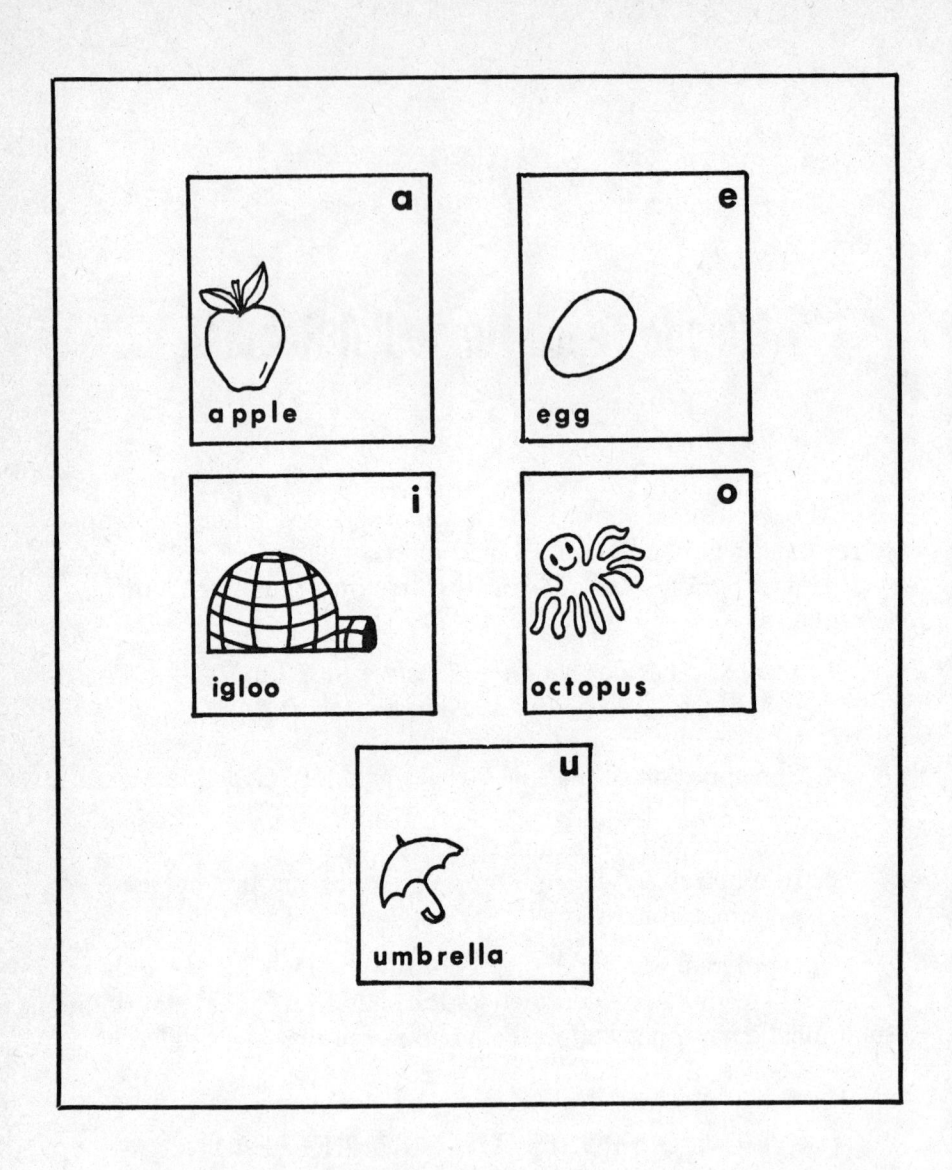

[Illustration: Five vowel picture cards — a/apple, e/egg, i/igloo, o/octopus, u/umbrella]

2. Make a set of colorful consonant and vowel sound cards. Be certain to place picture at left, letter at right side of card. Also, letters should be at the same distance from top margin on each card. 5″ x 8″ plain white index cards may be used. Cover with clear contact paper so they last.

How to Teach Remedial Reading 153

b — ball	c — car
d — door	f — fish
g — gate	h — house
j — jack-in-the-box	k — kite
l — lamp	m — moon

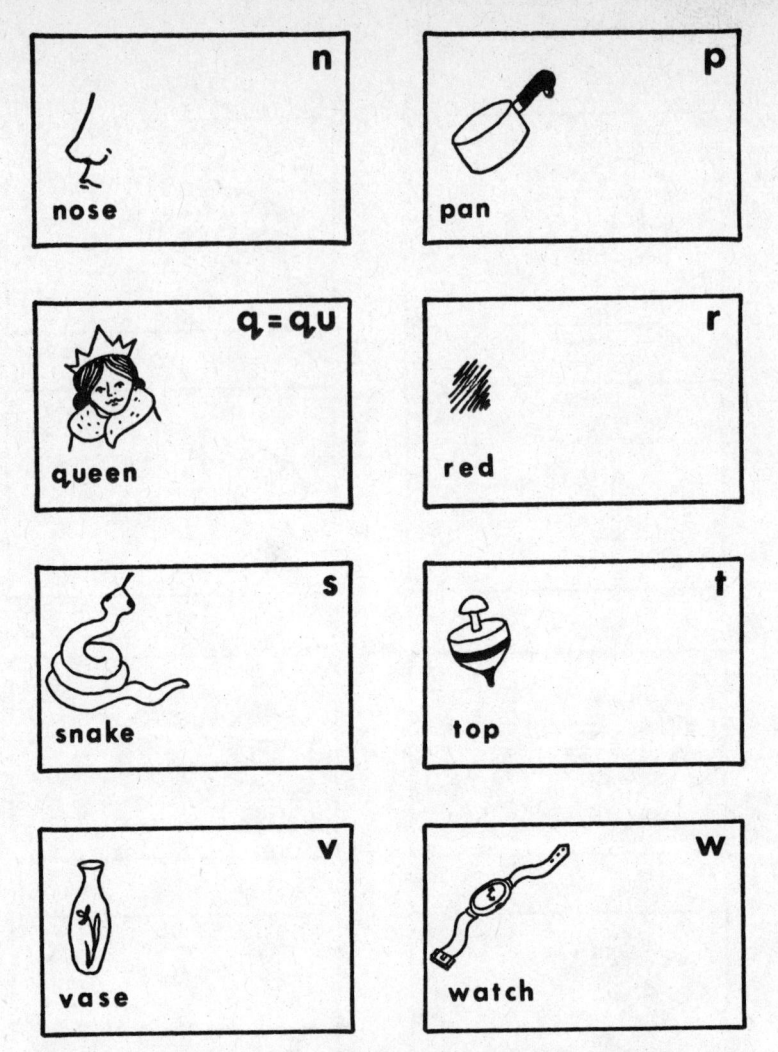

n — nose	**p** — pan
q = qu — queen	**r** — red
s — snake	**t** — top
v — vase	**w** — watch

Note: Teach *c* as the *k* sound; teach *g* as the *g* in *go*.

Note: Y is omitted for it has 3 sounds depending on position in the word. Z is rarely used so no card is necessary.

When you prepare the *r* card, take a red marker and color just above the word *red*.

3. You may want to put these vowels and consonants each on a ditto (one picture—one sound per ditto) and have the student make his own set of cards. (This is a seat work task enjoyed by many *young* LD children.) If you have the child do this task, make certain an older student or person sits with the child. The child should be asked to

repeatedly make the sound while he is coloring. The child should be asked for the object referent several times. Say, "*a* (sound) as in what?" child responds "Apple." You overemphasize *a* as you say *a*pple (unblend word by exaggerating *a* sound).

Note: If child makes his own set, introduce no more than 4 sounds in a day.

Note: When teaching *b*, *d*, be careful to make only the plosive noise. Do not say *buh* or *duh*, just *b*, *d* with a short blast of air escaping from the lips. Have child repeat sound repeatedly. If you are working with an auditorily handicapped child you will need to show him where to place his tongue and lips. Have him look at your mouth while you make the sound and feel the amount of air you use to make the sound.

DAY-BY-DAY ACTIVITIES

Day 1. Introduce sounds *a, b, c, d*.
- Children color ditto for each sound, saying sound as they color.
- Put down

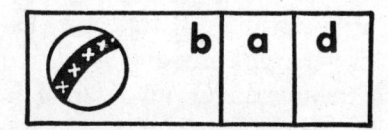

Pointing to *b*, say *b* sound. Move finger to *a*, make *a* sound. Move finger to *d*, make *d* sound. Pointing to each letter in sequence, blend letters together more rapidly until they close into the one syllable sound *bad*. Tell the children each letter in the word has a sound. Unblend the word again *b..a..d*. Ask each child in the group *(there should never be more than 4 children in a remedial group)* to point to each letter, make its appropriate sound then to say *b.a.d* slowly.
- Give each child a slip of paper with the word bad in 1" high letters. They trace each letter.

- Next work on language development. (Make sure children are *attentive*—looking at the board.) Ask them to look at the sentences you write. They are to find the word they just practiced in each one.

Note: Be sure to write sentences in manuscript. Books are printed, so you should be careful to form your letters carefully.

   1. The food tasted bad.
   2. The bad dog tore up the doll.
   3. When I was sick I felt bad.
   4. The rain came at a bad time.

Note: Have each child take a turn finding the word bad. Circle it. When all 4 *bads* have been located read the sentences to them. Then ask each child to orally make his own sentence using bad.

Day 2. Reinforce *a, b, c, d* sounds.

- Place letters one at a time on table as child makes sound ⓑ..ⓐ..ⓓ. Shove cards together. They say *bad*.
- Now reverse cards putting ⓓⓐⓑ. Ask "Is this word bad?" Regardless of answers, go through sounds *d ... a ... b*. Close them to *dab*. With your finger put a dab of paint on a card and say "This spot is a dab of paint."
- Now put down *c..a..b*. Ask if anyone can work it out. If someone can, reward him with "Super" or "That's great."
- Next try ⓑ ⓐ ⓒ. Do not add "k" at this point since you have not introduced it.
- Put ⓐⓓ down. Once it is named, show them an ad in the paper and say, "Mother wants to sell an old couch. She put an ad in the paper." Have a newspaper handy to demonstrate an "ad" sheet.)
- Have children write *bad* again. Follow this with a ditto (one per child). They circle each *bad*. Print on ditto should be large.

   1. The robbers were bad men.
      (skip space)
   2. It is a bad idea to throw rocks.
      (skip space)
   3. Put a dab of paint on this paper.
      (skip space)
   4. If I am bad, I get punished.

Day 3. Reinforce *a, b, c, d,* sounds and add the *e* (short sound).

- Have each child write *bad* 3 times, say word unblended and then closed.
- Give *e* ditto. They color, making "e" sound as *egg* repeatedly while coloring. Get individual feedback to be sure it sounds like *e*, not *i* or *a* as in *igg* or *agg*. It may be necessary to help auditorily handicapped child (looking in mirror) to get his mouth muscles placed right. Practice *e* sound.
- Now place *b a d* cards on table and *b e d* cards under *bad*. Ask if the words are just alike. Make sure each child sees that the middle letter is not the same.
Pointing to *bad* say "bad."
Pointing to *bed* say "bed."
Ask one child to make a sentence for *bad;* ask another child to make a sentence for *bed*.
- Give children a ditto with this on it.

![bed/bad overlapping letters illustration]

They say "bed."
- Show flash cards with these words. Ask each child to try to work out each word.

bad   dab   cab
bac   bed   ad

Shuffle cards between children.

Day 4. Reinforce *bad, bed,* and add *f.*

- Give each child a sheet of paper with yesterday's words on it. (Make the arrangement on each sheet different.)

dab	bed
bad	ad
cab	bac

bed	bac
bad	cab
dab	ad

etc.

As you say the word ask each child to point to the word you said. Watch carefully. If a child looks at his neighbor's paper, tell him his neighbor does not have the same words. If child cannot locate word, review Day 2 lesson with that child as soon as you can.
- Give *f* ditto. Children color it making *f* sound repeatedly.
- Show f|e|d today. Work it out—unblended, blended.
- Do language development.
  Put a few raisins in each child's mouth and say "I fed (child's name) raisins" end with "I fed my dog a bone."
- Have children write
  bed
  fed
  Ask "How these words are alike? How different?"
- Practice *bad* by writing it.

Day 5. Review *a, b, c, d, e, f,* sounds and add *g* as in *go*.
- Showing the *a, b, c, d, e, f* cards one at a time, children make sound (in unison) for each. After the *a* sound is given, ask for referent *apple*. After the *b* sound, ask for referent *ball*, and so on with each letter.
- Introduce *g* sound. Do not say *guh*, just let air out. Children color gate, making *g* sound repeatedly as they do.
- Put down cards b|a|g. See if children can work it through. Show a paper bag. Have it blown up, tied at top. (At *end* of the lesson play a game "What's in the bag?" Put some treat in it, such as a cookie. Give *clues* until someone wins it. Have an extra cookie or two in case there is a tie.
  Note: Occasionally during reading, add some fun so these turned-off children learn to regard reading period as a pleasant experience.
- Put down b|e|g. Reward first child to work it out. Do language development lesson with *beg*.
  "I will beg mother to let me go to the _____." Each child tells where he'd like to go.
  Then have each child role-play begging to go (you be the mother). Make them laugh with the "pretty please" routine.
- Have children compare b a g for likenesses and difference.
  b e g

Day 6. Review *b, c, d, f, g* sounds; reinforce *a* and *e*.
- Give dittos for each sound. Ask children to look at the first ditto

How to Teach Remedial Reading 159

and find all the things that begin with the letter *b*. After all the *b* items are located, give a simple ditto for *d*.

These dittos are easy to make. If you can't draw, cut pictures from old workbooks and paste on a sheet or check with your district for availability of this type of expendable materials.[12]
- Review sound of *a* and *e* with each child.

Day 7. Introduce "h" sound and review previously learned sounds.
- Give ditto of *h* (house). Have children color and repeat *h* sound as they do.
- Show *h a d* . Have them work it out, unblended then blended.
- Tell them you are going to play a game with some "silly words." Tell them these are not real words but just groups of sounds. This is an excellent test to determine which children need further review on all sounds to date. If a child gets the word you show him, let him keep the flashcard. Don't allow any one child to monopolize the game. See that all get several turns. Use the following non-sense words

  1. bef   4. feb   7. heb
  2. haf   5. gad   8. af
  3. gab   6. fab   9. hag

- Give them a ditto with several objects which begin with *h*. Have them circle those *h* words.

---
[12]First talking *Alphabet Duplicating Masters*. Scott-Foresman Co., Masters. Scott-Foresman Co., 1967.

Day 8. Introduce two sounds for *i*, *I* that refers to the person and the short *i* as in *if*.

- Write this sentence on the board.

    I had a bag.

    Even though these are remedial students someone will probably be able to read the sentence. Be sure to allow ample time for decoding. Let the silence be a little uncomfortable. If no one can decode sentence, read it to them. Ask what you mean by *I*. Develop the concept that stands for the person by putting a different object in each child's hand and having them say "I have a <u>name object.</u>" Objects they can keep are neat—a pencil, an apple, an eraser, a ball.

    Extend this activity thusly: Have the first child say "<u>I</u> have a pencil and I can write with it." Put this sentence on the board as child repeats it (Print and underline <u>I</u>). Second child says "<u>I</u> have an apple and I can eat it." Put sentence on board underlining I and so on until each child has participated.

- Introduce small *i* as in *if*. Tell them the little *i* says *i* as in *if*. Have them repeat sound several times. Have them listen for "i" and "f" in "if." When they hear "i," put up one finger; put up second finger as soon as they can hear "f."
- Put cards down for did . Work it out. Now show dad . Ask "Are these words alike? How are they different?"
- Give each child a slip with *did* and *dad* to say as they trace.

    did   dad

    Have them overemphasize the vowel sound as they say the words.
- Now put this sentence up:

    dad had a bag.

    Read it together.
- Practice spelling words, *had, bad, dad, bed, fed, did, if, big* by putting them on a ditto. The child traces a word, writes each letter in the middle column, then writes the word as a unit in the right column.

1. had ___ ___ ___

2. bad ___ ___ ___

3. dad ___ ___ ___

4. bed ___ ___ ___

5. fed ___ ___ ___

6. did ___ ___ ___

7. if ___ ___

8. big ___ ___ ___

Ask the children to say the first word aloud *"had."* Tell them to "Trace over had" (make sure they do), "Write it in the blanks, one letter per blank," "Write it freehand." Be sure no one rushes ahead to the next word.

Do the next word *bad* using the same instructions.

Do the next word *dad* using the same instructions.

Then ask what *had, bad,* and *dad* have in common. The children need to learn to see that the words rhyme because of the common ending.

Proceed through all 8 items as you did 1, 2, 3. Have them note that 4 and 5 have a common ending.

Day 9. Reinforce all words learned to date.

- Give each child a small roll of clay and a ditto of spelling words (same words as yesterday). The child names the word, writes it twice, then rolls it out using ropes of clay to form letters. After child shows word to you, take the index finger of the hand *he* uses to write and rub his fingers over each letter as he says *h .. a .. d.* Then have him say the word. Use this procedure until he has practiced each word in writing, in clay and by feeling the clay.

Day 10. Reinforce spelling words and give spelling pretest.

- Give each child a ditto like the one on page 161.
  Go through spelling words in manner described earlier.
- Ask each child to orally make a sentence for each word.
- Pretest all eight words. Ask each child to write the words. Say the word, give a sentence using the word, say the word again. After you check the words, children practice any missed words using the clay spelling technique.

Day 11. Review and test spelling, and introduce sound of *j*.

- Pretest spelling. Provide review clay practice on any missed word.
- Test spelling. Reward 100% with treat and praise.
- Introduce *j* sound. Have children color ditto saying "j" sound repeatedly as they do.
- Put j a b cards out—unblend and close it.
- Do word concept development. "I jabbed myself with a pencil. She jabbed me in the ribs with her elbow" (demonstrate on a kid). Ask, "What does jab mean?" Help them say it means to "poke at."

Day 12. Introduce *k* and *l* sounds, relating the sound of *k* to *c* sound.

- Color *k* picture saying *k* sound repeatedly.
- Color *l* picture making *l* sound repeatedly.
- Work out words l a b   f e l l   l e g   and   g a l .
- Test sounds learned so far. Say *g* sound. Ask them to write letter you said on paper. Skipping around, give all sounds *a* to *l*.

Day 13. Review *a* to *l* and introduce *m* and *n* sounds.

- Showing cards, have children give sound and object referent for each sound *a-l*.
- Color *m* ditto today having children make *m* sound as they do.
- Color *n* ditto (outline nose) saying *n* sound as they do.
- Put out cards m a n . Unblend it, then close it.
- Change it to c a n . Let someone work it out.
- Give each child a slip; they trace over *man, can*.
- Put this sentence on board. Caution children not to shout out. When they can read it they should raise their hand.

       A man hid a can in a bag.

Make a game of this. Go to the far side of the room and call the children one at a time to whisper the sentence to you.
Note: Children who are able to work it out without help are doing very well. Help those who are struggling to work it out, but also make a note of child's name and the letter giving that child trouble so you can help each child better in future lessons.
If time remains, do the same with *mad*.

Day 14. Review letters, introduce sound of *o*, give new spelling list.

- Show *a-n* cards; children name sound and object referent.
- Give ditto of *o*; have children repeat *o* sound as they color octopus.
- Put cards down d o g . They work it out.
  Change it to f o g .
  Change it to j o g .
  Change jog to j o b .
- Do a concept and language development lesson for *job*, meaning chore.
  "My job at home is to _____."
  Each child tells a chore he does to help at home.

- Give ditto of this week's spelling. Go through it as you did with last spelling lesson. This week's words are *and, dog, in, man, can, on, hill.*

Day 15. Help children practice this week's spelling list with clay, and give the first dictation lesson.

- Review cards *a-o;* children give sound and referrent.
- Give ditto of spelling words. Each child rolls one word at a time in clay, traces its letters with finger and calls them to you, says word.
- Give each child a ditto that looks like this:

1. A̲ m̲a̲n̲ h̲a̲d̲ a̲ d̲o̲g.

2. A̲ d̲o̲g h̲i̲d̲ i̲n̲ a̲ l̲o̲g.

- Tell the children you are going to say some words they know and they will write them one letter to a space.
- Read the following sentences one word at a time; don't go to the next word until you have guided each child to putting letters in the correct space. Since dictation is a new skill, you must help them. When you are finished each child's paper will look like this:

1. __ ____ ____ __ ____.

2. __ ____ ____ __ __ ____.

- If a small *a* has been used at the start of each sentence explain that the first word of a sentence must always begin with a capital letter. Have them change it.
- If some bright child asks how a dog can get in a log you need to explain about "hollow" logs. The toilet paper tube can serve as an illustration. Put a paper dog inside it. Be sure the children all know what a log is.

Day 16. Practice spelling list and introduce sound of *p.*

- Practice spelling words by tracing them one time; then ask

How to Teach Remedial Reading

children to try to spell them from memory (*on, hill, and, man, dog, can, in*).
- Introduce *p* sound; children color ditto saying *p* sound repeatedly.
- Put the following words on flash cards, and going round-robin see if the children can work them out:

    map, cap, mop, lap, nap
    pan, fan, fin, hop, l<u>and</u>
    h<u>and</u>, b<u>and</u>.

Let the child who gets word right keep flash card.

Day 17. Review and give test on this week's spelling words, and review all sounds to date.
- Give second dictation experience using these sentences and the ditto procedure described on page 164.

    1. I can hop.
    2. A man had a cap.

- If any child capitalized the first word of each sentence without being told, reward that child with some nuts or raisins. This gesture will serve as motivation to other children in the group. As you hand the reward to the child say "Tommy, thank you for capitalizing the first word of each sentence."

Day 18. Introduce sounds of *r* and *s* (for the moment we will skip "*q*" since "*q*" is always *qu*).
- Color *r*—red, say *r* sound repeatedly.
- Relate [red] to [bed] for its likeness and difference.
- Color *s* say "*s*" sound repeatedly.
- Put the following words on the board:
  and hill in man lap sip big
  Next begin listing rhyming words below each category. Ask children to name rhyming word round robin.

and	hill	in	man	lap	sip	big
band	kill	fin	ran	map	hip	pig
hand	fill	sin	fan	gap	lip	dig
sand	pill	pin	pan	snap	dip	fig
land	mill		can			

Day 19. Review all sounds to date, and give third dictation lesson.

- Put yesterday's rhyming words on flashcards. Shuffle them. Going round-robin, let children try a card, keep it if they say it correctly.
- Give each child a ditto to take dictation. Provide one space per letter. The first sentence is:

A̲ b̲i̲g̲ p̲i̲g̲ i̲s̲ i̲n̲ the s̲a̲n̲d̲.

In the above sentence you will supply *the* on the ditto. Thusly

1. __ ____ ____ ___ ___ the _____.

since you have not taught that word.
The next sentence is

A̲ man̲ ran̲ down a̲ hill̲.

On the ditto supply *down* since it has not been taught.

2. __ _____ _____ down __ _____.

The last sentence is

I will hand a fan to mom.

On the ditto supply *to*.

3. __ _____ _____ _ ____ to ____.

The children should be able to spell *mom* if you unblend it for them sound by sound.

Day 20. Introduce the sound of *t*.

- Give *t* ditto. The children will repeat the *t* sound many times while coloring it.
- Using the board, put up these letters one at a time; make a pause between words so children have time to think of sound.

　　　　　r .. a .. t

When someone yells "rat," say, "Good." "Now this time, don't say the word out loud, you can whisper it to me."

　　　　　g .. a .. s
　　　　　t .. o .. p

They whisper it.

- Give each child a set of flashcards to decode independently.

How to Teach Remedial Reading

Child A's List	Child B's List	Child C's List	Child D's List
1. rag	let	sit	has
2. get	hit	mad	fit
3. dog	tag	met	pet
4. bit	stab	lot	mop
5. stop	stop	pond	fast

The above exercise allows you to check progress of children. If the child decodes all 5 cards, he's doing well. If he can't, give that child more attention in your teaching.

Day 21. Introduce new spelling list and review all sounds to date.

- New spelling list will be on a tracing ditto. Use these words: *got, get* (have children compare these words for likeness, difference), *has, hat* (compare for likeness and difference), *not, hot* (compare for likeness and difference), *it, is.*
- Put these sentences on board. Let each child read one sentence.

    1. It is hot.
    2. A cap is a hat.
    3. Get a mop.
    4. I did not drop it.

Day 22. The children will practice spelling with clay and take fourth dictation lesson. Words underlined should be supplied on student ditto. Others can be unblended.

   1. I lost <u>my</u> top.
   2. I will beg mom <u>for</u> it.
   3. I sat on <u>my</u> hat.
   4. A cat is not as big as a dog.

- Reward, with an edible reward, any child who remembers to capitalize the first word of all sentences. Some child may take exception with sentence #4. That is good. Discuss the validity of the statement.

Day 23. Review spelling list with tracing ditto; pre-test spelling.

- Put these sentences on the board and ask each child to read one.

    1. A fat cat sat on a mat.
    2. A cat can kill a rat.

3. A man got mad at his dog.
4. I ran fast.

Day 24. Review, then test spelling. Introduce the sound of *u*.

- Children make *u* sound as in *us* as they color umbrella.
- Tell the children that today they will add two useful words to their spelling list: *up, us*.
- Practice *up* and *us* by tracing them.

Day 25. Review all sounds to date and reinforce the "u" sound. Give 5th dictation lesson.

- Show cards *a-u*; have children say sound, name object referent.
- Write these words on board.

    cut   cup   must
    but   tub   just
    nut   rub

    Work the words out.
- Give dictation ditto, with one blank per letter to each child. Supply the word *the*. Other words should be unblended until child gets them.

    1. I got in the tub.
    2. My hand is cut.
    3. The cup is not on the bed.
    4. I must help mom.

- Reward children who remember to capitalize first word of each sentence.

Day 26. It is time to introduce several much needed words.

- Prepare a tracing ditto with these words

    be , me , he , the , we

    Ask what the words have in common. Get the answer *e*. Say the words for the children emphasizing and exaggerating the *e* that says $\bar{e}$.
- Practice writing the words. Make a game of it.
- Give each child a card with two sentences on it to be decoded and read.

    Child A
    1. He is not as big as me.

2. We will be bad.

Child B
1. The cat ran up the hill.
2. He will get mad at me.

Child C
1. We must let the man help us.
2. He will put the cup up.

Child D
1. He can help me.
2. We will be on the last bus.

Day 27.

- Using tracing spelling and clay-rolled spelling, review *me, be, we, he, the*. Add *she* and teach *sh* sound.

  My aide adopted a term for sounds like *sh, th* and *ch*. She called them "peanut butter" sounds. She drew an analogy which the children loved and adopted. She reminded them that if you put peanut butter on bread it sticks so tight, you can't pull the peanut butter off without tearing the bread. She told them *s* and *h* when side by side are glued together and get a new sound *sh*. Then she put a finger to her lips and said "sh . h . h." All the children had the *sh* sound.

- Today add some new words on board.

  *sh*ut *sh*op *sh*ip *sh*ot *sh*ell

  The children by now will be feeling some prowess in decoding.

Day 28.

- Review *be, he, me, we, she* and *the* spelling list.
- Give sixth dictation lesson. Use sentences you put on Day 26 cards. Give the children a ditto with the correct number of blanks.

Day 29.

- Review and pretest spelling of *we, me, be, he, she, the*.
- Introduce *v* sound. As they color *v* ditto, they will repeat sound.
- Introduce *w* sound. As they color *w* ditto, they will repeat sound.
- Review all sounds with cards. The children have now learned

all alphabet sounds except *qu, x, y, z*. These can be added later.

Day 30.

- Review and test spelling.
- Give the following sentences as dictation. Today do not give children a ditto. Let them write sentences on lined paper.

  1. A man ran up to me.
  2. I will get a dog.
  3. On top of the hut is a cat.
  4. We fan if it is hot.
  5. A cat has soft fur.

Day 31.

- Teach peanut butter sound *th*. For the auditorily handicapped child, have child stick tongue out with upper teeth resting on top of the tongue and force air out around the sides of the tongue.
- Have children practice the following useful words:

  this   that   them

- Ask children to promise not to shout out the word you are going to put on the board. Tell them you will reward them if they whisper it to you. Put up *both*. If someone does shout it out, reward all the other children but do not give shouter a reward. Say to the children who did not shout, "I'm giving you the cookie because I'm sure you would have gotten it if you had had a chance." Do not fuss at the shouter. Let the matter drop there.

Day 32. Reinforce sounds and give another dictation lesson.

- Put several cut out sandpaper letters in a bag. Without looking and by feel the child will choose a letter and name as many words as he can that start with the letter. He gains 1 point per word he can spell. List words on board. (Letters in bag will be *s, t, h, c, f.*
- The dictation sheet will have one blank per letter. Unknown words should be supplied.

  1. The cat ran from the dog.
  2. It ran up a tree.
  3. A man had to get it down.
  4. He got mad at the dog.
  5. I held the cat on my lap.

How to Teach Remedial Reading

Day 33. Teach *no, so, go, to, do*.

- Give tracing ditto with these words. As children trace say word. Ask at the end "What do all these words have in common?" Answer "end in o."
- Give ditto like this:

Read statement. Answer <u>yes</u> or <u>no</u>
1. Can a cat sit?
2. Do cans run?
3. Is the sun hot?
4. Can I get in the tub?
5. Is it fun to get a cut?
6. Will I get a tan if I sit in the sun?
7. Can I go to bed?

- Make sure each child reads each question aloud to you. Thus you can check decoding progress to date and give help to lagging students.

Day 34. Introduce an all-important rule. Structure lesson carefully and demand attention.

- Write this rule on the board:
  "When a word ends with <u>e</u>, the <u>e</u> makes the other vowel say its name."
- Tell the children they are about to learn something very important so they must listen very carefully. Read the rule three times.
- Put up these examples under the rule:

  | us | at | rip | hop | pet |
  | use | ate | ripe | hope | pete |

- Have children read <u>us</u>. Point to the e in <u>use</u>. Draw a circle around e and an arrow back to u ū s ⓔ
  Say "The <u>e</u> on the end makes the <u>u</u> say its name ū. This word is <u>use</u>.
  Have the children repeat <u>us</u> as you point at it and <u>use</u> as you point. Ask "Why did the <u>u</u> in <u>use</u> say its name?" The answer is "Because of the <u>e</u> on the end."

- Point to the at. Have children say it. Circle e and draw an arrow back to "a." a t e. "This word is ate. I ate my carrots. What did the e do to the a?" Wait for answer.
- Follow same procedure with each word.
- At the end put up a word for each child.
  Child A—kit "Now change it to kite."
      Child puts an e on the end.
  Child B—tim "Now change it to time."
      Child adds e.
  Child C—pan "Now change it to pane,
      I broke the window pane."
      Child adds e.
  Child D—cut "Now change it to cute."
      Child adds e.
- Ask children round-robin to decode. Give help as needed. Make child repeat rule.

    h o m e   p i e
    c a k e   l i k e
    c a m e   m i n e
    f i r e   r o p e

Day 35. Reinforce rule regarding e on end and give new spelling words.

- Review rule for e. Have them decode these words (2 per child).

    came five gave hide made
    nine ride take home bike

- Review
  mad goes to made because of e. hid goes to hide because of e.
- Give new spelling list. Include
  mad, made
  hid, hide
  ask, but
  do, to
  Trace words and say them.

Day 36.

- Study spelling list, orally give sentences for words, and have another dictation lesson. Have children write on paper with spaces for each letter.

1. I w<u>i</u>ll g<u>o</u> t<u>o</u> b<u>e</u>d.
2. H<u>e</u> w<u>i</u>ll h<u>e</u>lp m<u>e</u>.
3. I g<u>o</u>t <u>u</u>p l<u>a</u>t<u>e</u>.
4. W<u>e</u> c<u>a</u>m<u>e</u> h<u>o</u>m<u>e</u>.
5. I w<u>i</u>ll r<u>i</u>d<u>e</u> <u>o</u>n a b<u>i</u>k<u>e</u>.

Day 37.

- Review spelling list and continue to work with "e on the end" rule. Give each child a slip of 3 sentences to decode and read to you.

    Child A
    1. I can go but I must be home at five.
    2. We can help mom.
    3. I like to go to the lake and swim.

    Child B
    1. Ask mom to bake a cake.
    2. It will not take long to make it.
    3. I like hot cake.

    Child C
    1. I like to jump rope.
    2. On a hot day I bathe the dog.
    3. He has a bike like mine.

    Child D
    1. Mom let us go to the store.
    2. We got a can of pop to drink.
    3. I had fun.

Day 38. Pretest spelling and introduce concept of vowels and consonants.

- Put rule on board

    "The vowels are a, e, i, o, u
       sometimes y and w."

    Have children repeat the rule several times.

- Give sheet with alphabet. Ask children to circle all vowels. Finished sheets should look like this:

    ⓐ b c d ⓔ f g h ⓘ j
    k l m n ⓞ p q r s t
    ⓤ v ⓦ x ⓨ

- Explain that any letter that is not a vowel is a consonant.
- Put these words on board

    tape seat woke table
    make soap pig coat

    Ask child to circle all the vowels in each word. Go over together.
- Give follow-up card to each child.
    The child circles each vowel.

Child A	Child B	Child C	Child D
jump	lead	see	dear
treat	tip	wig	turn
open	meet	seat	fix

Day 39. Review spelling, take test. Review consonant-vowel lesson giving another exercise like the last one yesterday. Explain that "every word has at least one vowel."

- Ask the children to find the vowels in these words on board. Discuss; try to work out words.

toe	long	best	must
pile	me	drop	tire

- Give dictation on lined paper with spaces for each word.
    1. S̲a̲m̲ i̲s̲ a̲ p̲i̲g̲.
    2. H̲e̲ l̲i̲k̲e̲s̲ m̲u̲d̲.
    3. H̲e̲ t̲a̲k̲e̲s̲ a̲ b̲a̲t̲h̲ i̲n̲ i̲t̲.
    4. H̲i̲s̲ s̲k̲i̲n̲ i̲s̲ covered w̲i̲t̲h̲ m̲u̲d̲.

Day 40. Introduce a new rule. It is important to have children's attention and have lesson well-structured. Provide for adequate feedback from each child.

- Put rule up

    "When a word has 2 vowels the first one says its name."
- Read rule 3 times and demonstrate:

    met (they say it)

    meat (show the ⓔⓐ)

    Explain the e̲ says e̅ and they can pretend the a̲ says nothing.

How to Teach Remedial Reading 175

Demonstrate:

ran becomes rain. Because of the i the ā says its name.

Demonstrate:

red becomes "read."
- Put up these words on board.

    day play keep see need

    Circle the a y in "day" pretend it is "da," making "a" say "ā." Go over each word.
- Provide for feedback individually with children.

Child A		Child B	
1. may	3. feet	1. tray	3. lead
2. way	4. seat	2. pray	4. boat
Child C		Child D	
1. say	3. coat	1. stay	3. goat
2. bay	4. train	2. hay	4. heat

Day 41. Review yesterday's lesson regarding two vowels side by side and reinforce concept through spelling list.

- This week's words are

play	heat
say	meat
may	seat
way	beat

- Make sentences orally with each word.

Day 42. Now the children are ready to be introduced to a book. Try to find a basal reader the child has never used before. (If a child has failed previously with a given book, he usually has a negative attitude toward it.) I personally like the Ginn 720 reading series because it has detailed directions for the teacher, built-in activities for students who need additional help, and enrichment activities for students who don't. Other possibilities for the first readers are the Readers Digest Series, Part 1 and the *I Can Read It Myself* books.

In introducing the book allow time for the children to thumb through it, looking at pictures. When they tire of this, thumb together page-by-page, picking out and listing words they can work out on the board. The purpose of this activity is to help the children realize they can now read many of the words.

Day 43. Plan your lesson carefully. If there are sight words like *come* or *look*, put them on a tracing ditto and go over them before starting the lesson.

Read the story to the children using good expression. Talk about what happens in the story. If there is a sequence of events, discuss what happened first, second, third. Enjoy the pictures.

Make sure each remedial child reads every story to you. If he misses a word make a note of it; include that word on his weekly spelling list, using clay spelling and tracing to teach it.

From the first story on, follow these principles:

GENERAL PRINCIPLES FOR TEACHING READING

Suggestion 1: **Make your instructional time with the child more productive.** This child needs quiet, uninterrupted, carefully structured reading sessions designed to hold his attention. Two 25 minute reading instruction sessions per day will usually be far more productive than one 1 hour session. Be careful not to introduce more than 3-4 elements in a given day and be certain to review and reinforce previously acquired elements or words. Remember the remedial child does not learn incidentally. Be sure to give sufficient reinforcement. The child should be required to read with a marker (an index card will do). Moving the card along helps to hold his attention. Reward good attention with a tangible reward.

Suggestion 2: **Insist upon accuracy.** If the book says "come home" don't let the child say "come here" even if it makes sense in context. Ask him to look at the word after "come" and spell it. He may correct his own mistake. If not tell him the correct word and review it with him at the end of the lesson.

Suggestion 3: **Don't be afraid to give help.** Children often need help with workbook questions. Help them get the right answer down (spelled correctly). *Then* discuss why the answer is correct. Build any necessary concepts. Watch for language development opportunities.

Suggestion 4: **Go slow. Work for mastery.** At the end of each reading lesson after each child has read the selection to you, give one or two follow-up dictation lessons utilizing the words and ideas from the story to make the dictation sentences.

Suggestion 5: **Try to develop good peer-relations within each group.** Nothing has more influence than when one child says to another "Hey, you're reading better." Respond to the complimenting child first, "That was a really nice thing to say, Sam." Then turn to the child who received the compliment and say, "He's right, you really have improved. That's great!" This kind of response on your part will keep the encouraging remarks coming and will become a definite motivator to the children.

Suggestion 6: **Use words from their reading for each week's spelling.** Add one or two words from competency tests (Chapter 3) each week.

Suggestion 7: **Program-in some fun.** Children love plays and memorizing short poems. If the children have trouble remembering the words, you can have them mime the actions while you act as narrator to do the words.

Use behavior modification (rewards) to encourage children to do their best and act appropriately.

Suggestion 8: **Always get feedback!**

HOW TO USE NEUROLOGICAL IMPRESS TO TEACH REMEDIAL READING

Before closing this chapter, it seems appropriate to mention a process called neurological impress. I have used this technique with older students and can attest to the fact it works with some children. This technique is a great one to use once a child is reading at a grade level of 2.0 or up.

First you need to obtain a set of cards you can use. At the end of this chapter are sample paragraphs that may be used. You will need an identical set for each remedial child. Use a copying machine. If it is at all possible, limit your remedial groups to 4 students. When you begin, there are some general principles to follow.

Have a reward system and a record-keeping system, and insist that each child use his finger to follow as another child reads.

On the first day pass out the sets of cards; say

"Take the rubber band off, place it on your wrist." Look to see if they do.

"Put your finger on the first word." Look to see if they do.

"Are you *ready*? I will read the card to you, then one of you will try to read it to me. Here we go. If you follow with your finger, you will get a _____." (I use peanuts)

Now you read the card slowly. Stop at each period. *Check to be sure they are moving their fingers.*

At the end ask your strongest reader to read it. Tell them that

- if the child needs help the teacher will give it.
- if their fingers follow each word, they will get a reward _____ (peanuts).

Ask "Are you ready?" After each child puts finger down, say to the reader, "Begin."

As the child reads, don't let him struggle. Supply any words he takes more than 5 seconds to decode. Count his errors, record words missed if less than 5, watch others to see their fingers move. When the card is finished reward followers, then say to the reader:

"Let's look at this word." (Choose one word he missed, preferably one he should have gotten.) Discuss why it is what it is, discuss rules he could have used to decode it.

Tell the child how many errors he made and tell him he will get a chance to read the same card the next day.

Proceed to card 2, following the same format. A different child reads.

Proceed to card 3, and so forth, letting each child have a turn.

If a child reads a card 100%, give him a double reward and allow him to try a second card that day. If the second card is also read correctly heap verbal praise on him. This builds confidence.

On the second day and subsequent days have each child continue to read his card until it's 100% accurate. Reward that child for a decrease in the number of errors and reward other children if they are following word-for-word with their finger.

As a child follows this closely, he is also learning these words. He is seeing/hearing them. When his time comes on that card, he may be word-perfect the first time.

As you talk to each child about a missed word and its rules, learning by the other group members should be occurring because they realize they *too* will eventually read that card and receive double reward for a correct reading the first time.

If you follow the step-by-step suggestions and utilize the techniques outlined in this chapter, you should achieve good results in both reading and spelling. Remember each child requires multiple exposures to a word before it is "learned." It is not unusual to have to expose the child 80-90 times before he knows a word (this is why neurological impress works).

Help the child to build units. In a word such as visit, help him see the "is" and the "it."

Teach syllabication rules:

C V C V = vowel, consonant, vowel
in words such as delay
             c v c v

Give him clues such as that the "e" is a long vowel because of the V C V rule and the "a" is long because the "y" is acting as a vowel; thus you have 2 vowels side by side.

V C/C V = vowel, consonant, consonant, vowel

By this rule words are syllabicated between the consonants. Begin with words like *big/ger* or *run/ning* but show the child it works with words such as *af/ter* or *on/ly*.

Assume nothing: do not teach incidentally. *Drill*

Make a point to repeatedly use the words you are trying to teach in the daily (or at least 3 times weekly) dictation lessons. In these lessons, save the papers and help each child center in on his mistakes.

By doing these things you will achieve outstanding results.

The teaching of remedial reading is a challenging and very rewarding experience. The step-by-step program outlined here has proven successful for me time after time. I'm sure it will work for you, too.

SAMPLE PARAGRAPHS FOR NEUROLOGICAL IMPRESS SESSIONS

1. Each year many people die from heart attacks. The heart is a small organ about the size of your fist. It pumps blood to all parts of your body. The heart beats between 60 and 100 times each minute. Jogging a little way each day builds a strong heart.

2. Some dogs are big. Some are little. Big dogs need to have a place where they can run and romp. Little dogs need protection and therefore need to live indoors. If a dog is kept inside, he should be taken for a walk every day.

3. All people have to clean their noses. Our nose gets full of dirt. Inside the nose are many hairs and a sticky substance which catches dirt as we take air in. When our nose is full we clean it. Manners teach us not to pick our noses in front of other people, and since it is dirt we are taking out, we should not eat it.

4. Everyone has problems. Each day we face situations where we must decide what to do. A little problem and one easy to resolve, is what to wear. A harder problem to solve is what to do about parents who hit too hard when they are angry. Sometimes it is a help to talk to a teacher or a minister if we have a big problem. Because these people are older and have lived longer, they know things children don't know yet.

5. You have five senses. They help you learn about the world. Your eyes help you see color, size, and shape. Your ears bring in the sounds of the world; for example, a screeching noise may be an owl or tires from a skidding car. Your nose catches smells; it will tell you if something is on fire. Your fingers help you tell coarse from smooth, oil from water. Your sense of taste brings you much enjoyment.

6. The sun is the center of our solar system. Around our sun are nine planets that we know about. It may be there are more. Pluto was only seen a few years ago. When we get stronger telescopes we may see another planet. The planets move around the sun in paths we call orbits. We do not feel this movement because we are used to it.

7. People need people. A friend is someone who cares about us. We can talk over our problems with this person. Some children do not know how to make a friend. They try to buy a friend by giving that person money or things. Sometimes they tease the person which is the wrong way to make a friend because it makes the other person mad. Sometimes all you have to do to make a friend is say, "I would like to be friends with you."

8. "Finder's keepers, loser's weepers." You have all said this from time to time. When you find something of value, it is easy to forget that someone has lost it and wants it back. On

the other hand, when you lose something, you look for it, you ask other people if they have seen it, and you hope you can find it. Wouldn't it be upsetting if you lost something and you knew someone found it, but they wouldn't give it back? Think about this the next time you find something.

9. A plant is alive just as you are. It eats by getting water and food from the soil. It takes in air through little holes in its leaves. It gets rid of waste by breathing out through these holes. Plants even move. Many of them will turn all the way around so they can face the sun or get more light.

10. Cats are said to have nine lives. They do not really have more than one life. Cats run very fast and usually can get out of the way of cars or trucks. They can also see very well and can hear sounds much better than people can. This helps them see danger in time to get away from it. Even when a cat is sleeping, he is more alert than a sleeping person. A sudden noise will make a cat jump to his feet.

11. Fall is the time of the year when school begins and the weather starts to cool down. The leaves on some trees change from their summer green to red, yellow or orange. As the weather gets cooler and winter nears, these trees lose their leaves. In winter these trees are bare.

12. Getting mad is hard on your body. Your stomach may hurt. Your head may hurt. When you feel this way it is a good idea to talk about how you feel. If you are angry at a person, go to him and say "I am really mad at you," then explain why you feel so angry. That person may tell you why he did or said whatever made you mad. You may find there has been a <u>mis</u> <u>un</u> <u>der</u> <u>stand</u> <u>ing</u>, and there was no reason for you to feel as you did. Or the other person may apologize so you can be friends again.

13. Smoking is a bad habit. If you have not started it, you won't have to quit it. It blackens the lungs and makes it harder for your body to get the air it needs. Your fingers stink. You burn holes in your clothes and furniture. It costs a lot of money. It is hard to understand why anyone would do it. Most smokers say they began to smoke because they wanted to look grown-up or because peers were smoking.

14. All things are made of tiny parts called molecules. For a long time scientists said molecules existed even though no one had ever seen one. Now, with powerful microscopes, we can see them. In solid things, like a desk, the molecules rub together. In liquids they are not so close together, and in gases the molecules are farther apart.

15. You will be hearing more and more about the "right to die." For hundreds of years doctors felt they should keep people alive as long as they could. Now dying people's hearts can be made to beat with modern machines, and they can be made to breathe—even when the brain is dead. Some people feel that it is wrong to use these machines. When the plug is pulled the person dies. Many well people are putting a statement in their wills saying they do not want these machines used on them if they become very ill.

16. Would you pay $110 dollars for a meal? There is a restaurant in Switzerland where you would. You may eat fish, fowl, cheese and eggs there but the way they are fixed is different. The food is put on the plates in designs. Colors are considered; you may be served a ring of green vegetables with an inner yellow egg ring and black fish in the center. Wine is what you drink. The main dish is fresh lobster. This is the best restaurant in the world.

17. The largest animal is the whale. While whales live in water and look like fish, they are mammals. Like man, the whale must surface to breathe, and if he can't he will drown. The baby whale nurses his mother. Whales make noises and seem to talk to each other with these sounds. Scientists want to learn more about what these noises mean. Someday we may be able to talk with whales if we can learn to decode these messages.

18. Children usually want their teachers to like them. They quickly learn that most teachers like the child who is a good listener, gets his work done on time, and really tries to do it right. They also figure out that the child who is noisy, has to be pushed <u>con stant ly</u> and does not care if it is right, is not going to be chosen for special jobs such as passing paper or going to the office. The reason for this is simple: it is easy for

the teacher to be nice to people who treat her with respect and courtesy.

19. Man has dreamed of flying for a long time. It was not until about seventy-five years ago that anyone did fly. The first airplane did not fly far. The men who made that first plane would be dumbfounded if they could see a modern jet plane. The people who hang-glide come as close to being birds as a person can. They glide off a cliff and glide on the air. By moving the body they make the hang-glider go right or left.

20. Boxing is a sport enjoyed by many people. To be a boxer a man must get his body in top shape. His training involves running, bending, lifting, climbing. He learns how to punch and how to be punched. When in the ring he wears safety helps to protect his teeth and stomach. One of the jobs of the referee is to stop a fight before a fighter is hurt badly. Some boxers make a lot of money on a fight.

21. An eagle is a large bird. The mother eagle and father eagle mate for life. When the babies come, there are two. The parents are kept busy finding and bringing the babies food, such as rats, rabbits and mice to eat. Later the babies have to learn to fly. At first they just stand in the nest and flap their wings. Soon they become strong and can lift their big bodies into the air.

22. Baking bread is quite an art. The flour, water, yeast and shortening must be mixed carefully. The baker kneads the bread dough and puts it in a warm place to rise. It puffs up because of bubbles made by the yeast. The baker then kneads the dough again, shapes it into loaves and sets it out to rise one more time. At last it is baked. Nothing tastes better than just-baked, warm bread spread with butter. Since breadmaking takes several hours, most people buy bread instead of making it.

11

How to Teach Remedial Arithmetic

In my experience about one in seven children encounters problems in math. The child who has problems with reading may also have problems with math, but not necessarily. I have concluded that the reason children have problems in math rests largely with how it is taught. In the early school experience we go *too* fast for some children. They lack the ability to visualize that the numbers stand for concrete objects. They are not given sufficient manipulative experience to gain this concept, i.e., numbers stand for objects. If you peruse elementary math textbooks you will find, in general, there are no more than 3-4 pages on a given concept—insufficient drill for the child with limited perceptual experiences or limited language development. Likewise, while many texts use pictorial presentation at these early stages, *which is essential*, the classroom teacher needs to supplement these experiences with manipulative experiences. The child who has played counting games with his parents or older siblings and who has been bombarded with TV programs such as the "Electric Company," may not have problems, but for the child who does not understand the concept that 5 steps are more than 4 steps or 7 beans make a smaller pile than 10 beans, math is a confusing jumble of nonsense symbols.

By the time this child reaches grade 2 or 3, he is lost. He doesn't really understand the meaning of the numbers 1-10, yet his text is demanding that he work with hundreds or in some cases thousands in complex processes involving joining sets or taking them apart. He probably has learned to hate math.

What is his prognosis? In my opinion he will never overcome his math handicap until we go back and work our way painstakingly through the numbers concept, the more/less concept and the manip-

How to Teach Remedial Arithmetic

ulative processes of "guesstimating" amounts and joining or separating amounts.

Therefore, I feel remedial math instruction will be a slow process at first but will pay off in the long run. The activities suggested in this chapter are sequential, but they involve much manipulative and pictorial experience.

Note: Guesstimating involves the teacher putting down various quantities of items—beans, blocks, sticks—and asking "How many do you think are there?" The child approximates the answer (prior to counting). This process must be repeated until he grasps 1-10, 10-100 and can come close to the correct amount by just looking at the size of the pile. It involves using items of varying sizes.

Skill 1. Teach the numbers 1-10.

1. Have the child learn to write these numbers sequentially. Use tracing activities as often as needed.
2. Have the child relate an amount to each number.

On day 1 you might have him use a ditto like the following.

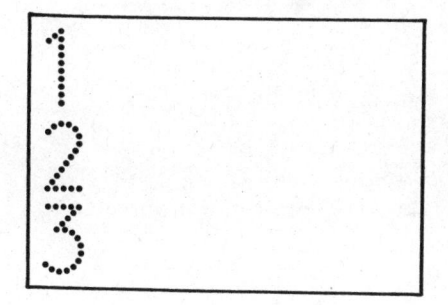

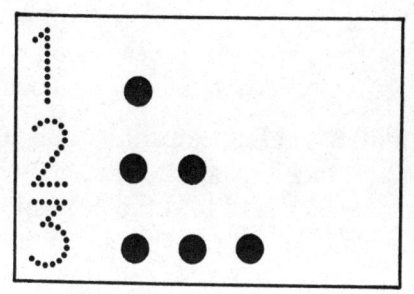

The child makes one dot, then 2 dots, then 3, and so on up to ten.

Your job is to help the child see that with each successive number, he is making 1 "more" dot.

Follow this activity by having the child put down a 1 (cut from cardboard), laying one block beside it; next he puts 2 down and demonstrates with 2 blocks. Have him look back at his 1 and see that 2 is 1 + 1. Continue this same process until he reaches 10.

On another day play a stepping game. Put cut out feet marked 1, 2, 3–10 on floor. Tell the child "to take" lets say "4 steps." When he is standing on four ask him what number is 1 more or 1 less or 2 more or 2 less. Continue this type of practice.

Follow this activity with a ditto where the child names the number that is one "greater" and the number that is one "less" than the given number.

Spill a small pile of beans before each remedial child. Ask him to count them. Add 1 more bean to each child's pile. Have him count again. Be sure he verbalizes "eight is one more than seven" or "six is one more than five."

Change mediums. Put a small pile of counting blocks before each child. Repeat counting activity adding 1 more and getting the child to verbalize what has been done.

Do the same activities removing a bean or block. This time the child expresses the "one less" concept.

On a different day use sticks to count "one more" or "one less." Be careful to get the child to verbalize "eight is one more than seven" or "five is one less than six." Use M and M's candies to do same activity.

Continue these kinds of activities on subsequent days using numbers 1–10 until each child can verbalize easily what he is doing. Next ask him to tell you "what number would be 2 more or 2 less." If he can do this without counting a concrete object, he has mastered the concept. If he can't, you must go through the same kinds of activities adding (more) or taking away (less) objects.

Skill 2. Adding sums less than 10.

Once the child can do the above he is ready to add sums which total less than 10. At the beginning, insist he draw or cut objects from magazines to prove his answers.

$$\begin{array}{r} 1 \\ +3 \\ \hline 4 \end{array} \bullet \;\; \begin{array}{r} 2 \\ +5 \\ \hline 7 \end{array} \bullet\bullet$$

Begin drill on sums less than 10.

Help the child understand that 1 + 3 is always 4, never anything different. Use a 5 minute drill with flash cards daily until members of the group have commited the facts 1-10 to memory.

Skill 3. Subtracting amounts less than 10.

Follow the same process in teaching subtracting with amounts less than 10.

Provide the child with pictorial dittoes. He crosses out the amount that is to be taken away.

How to Teach Remedial Arithmetic

```
  7
- 3
───
  4
```

∨ ∨ ∨ ∨ ∨ ∨

Commit the subtraction facts 1-10 to memory by flashcard drill. Teach the inter-relationship of addition and subtraction.

```
  3      4      7      7
+ 4    + 3    - 3    - 4
───    ───    ───    ───
  7      7      4      3
```

Begin stating horizontally as well as vertically.

3 + 4 = 7
4 + 3 = 7
7 − 3 = 4
7 − 4 = 3

Provide the child with at least 2 to 3 days practice using concrete objects to prove the associative quality of adding and subtracting.

Skill 4. Teach fractions concept of half a group.

Example: Tell the child to put out four checkers—show him half; write the word half—HALF—for him; write the symbol—½. With manipulations (beans/checkers), have him show you half of 6. This type of activity may take many repetitions, but it is important. If the child does not understand after ten explanations, use a piece of rope or card or two circles made from construction paper to help.

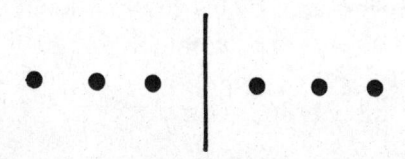

● ● ● | ● ● ●

After the children have the concept of half, put out 3 checkers; ask, "what is half?" Talk about the process of having to divide a whole in half.

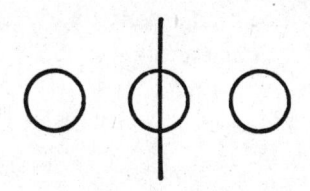

O ⏀ O

Give manipulative practice dividing odd numbers as well as even numbers in half. Briefly introduce the idea of half dollars by explaining that we can't cut a dollar bill in half, but we use coins (show half dollar) to get parts of a dollar. Have the children feel it and look at both sides (this is an exposure experience).

Skill 5. Teach the child to count from 1-100. Show the child how it goes, using a ditto like this:

```
0   1   2   3   4   5   6   7  8   9
10  11  12  13  14  15  16  17 18  19
20  2_  2_  2_  2_  2_
3_  3_  _
4_
5_
```

Help the child see as he progresses down each row the initial number is one more than the previous row.

This counting activity will take about 2 weeks if it is done daily. Have the child fill out the ditto each day 1-100 and have him move his finger from number to number as he calls its name.

During this two weeks accompany the above drill with guesstimating and counting activities using manipulative objects: checkers, blocks, pennies, popsicles sticks, etc. Vary the counting objects every 2 or 3 days.

Skill 6. Teach the child to add numbers 1-100 using concrete experiences with manipulatives.

Put out 13 checkers and 15 checkers, for example, Have the child count them when the sets are joined.

This is a good time to also show nim if he begins with 28 checkers and takes 13 away, he gets 15.

$$13 + 15 = 28$$
$$15 + 13 = 28$$
$$28 - 13 = 15$$
$$28 - 15 = 13$$

Provide several of these manipulative experiences before going to pencil and paper activities that involve adding. When you do go to pencil and paper activities make sure that for the first 7-10 days the numbers do not involve carrying.

This would be a good time to expose the child to a calendar. He needs to *learn:*

How to Teach Remedial Arithmetic

1. What it is called—"a calendar"
2. What it can be used for—to count the days 1-30 or 1-31 or 1-28/29 depending on the month, and it can be used to see how long it is until a holiday, such as a birthday or Halloween (Christmas, etc.)
3. To name the 7 days in proper sequence.
4. The calendar can be used as a number-line to add and subtract.

Skill 7. Teach place value—ones and tens.

Help the child see that 27 is 2 sets of 10 sticks (rubber band the sets of 10) and 7 loose sticks.

Give multiple manipulative experiences with place value until the child can tell you how many tens and ones are in any number 1-100. (100 being 10 sets of 10).

Skill 8. Teaching counting by 10's to 100.

10 - 20 - 30 - 40 - 50 - 60 - 70 - 80 - 90 - 100

Present it this way also:

```
   10            10
 + 10            10
   20          + 10
                 30
```

Skill 9. Introduce concept that a dime stands for 10. Give practice counting money. Have children handle real money so they can feel its weight, see faces on both sides.

Skill 10. Teach the child to add numbers where the sum will be less than 99 and carrying is involved. Provide manipulative materials such as sticks (rubber-banded in groups of 10) and where the single sticks can be banded to form 1 additional group of 10. *Show* him repeatedly how this is done, first manipulatively and then on paper.

```
    1             1
   25            19
 + 16          + 18
    1             7
```

When you begin showing him how to carry on paper, make the child prove a few of his answers to you using manipulatives (tens + regrouping of ones into banded 10). Examples:

```
  23          14          17
+ 19        + 26        + 28
```

Continue these manipulative and paper and pencil activities until you are satisfied the child knows the concept. (The only way you can know for sure is to listen to him explain it to you and the group). Counting pennies and adding varying amounts of pennies fascinates kids.

Skill 11. Teach subtracting without borrowing (with manipulative back-up) until mastered.

Skill 12. Teach subtracting that involves borrowing using sticks (banded into groups of 10). By this manipulative experience he must "spill" a set of 10 to see why we move the 1 from the tens place to the ones place to do this operation.

Go slow. Keep doing the manipulative experience of unbanding and spilling an extra 10 until the child's verbalizations and pencil and paper activities show he has the concept.

Skill 13. Introduce real coins—real pennies with the value of one, real nickels with the value of five, real dimes with the value of 10 and real quarters with the value of 25.

Using real money, allowing time to feel, look at, compare, teach children to count sums of money up to 99¢.

A ditto which shows the numbers 1 to 99 is helpful. For example if child lays down a nickel he puts an X on the 5. When he puts a second nickel down, he counts 5+5 on ditto so he can see the movement (just as he did walking off 1-10 on feet on the floor). Follow a similar procedure with a quarter and a dime. Have him mark the 25 with an X and move forward 10 spaces. On paper demonstrate 25
+ 10
so he sees how paper answers relate to the movement on his counting ditto.

Vary the money amounts. Give each child sufficient chances to demonstrate what he is doing until you are sure the concept is mastered.

Skill 14. Teach child to use a foot ruler and a yard ruler. A ruler can be used as a number line to demonstrate 6 + 5 = 11, or on the yardstick 18 + 10 can be demonstrated.

How to Teach Remedial Arithmetic

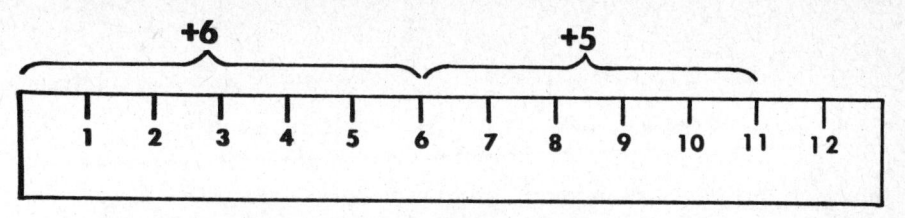

Give the concrete experiences of drawing lines which are a given number of inches long as well as measuring the length of certain objects.

Skill 15. Teach multiplication by relating it to the process of adding.

3 + 3 = 6 but so is 2 groups of 3 things = 6 things.

Using a rope to surround each group use manipulatives to demonstrate

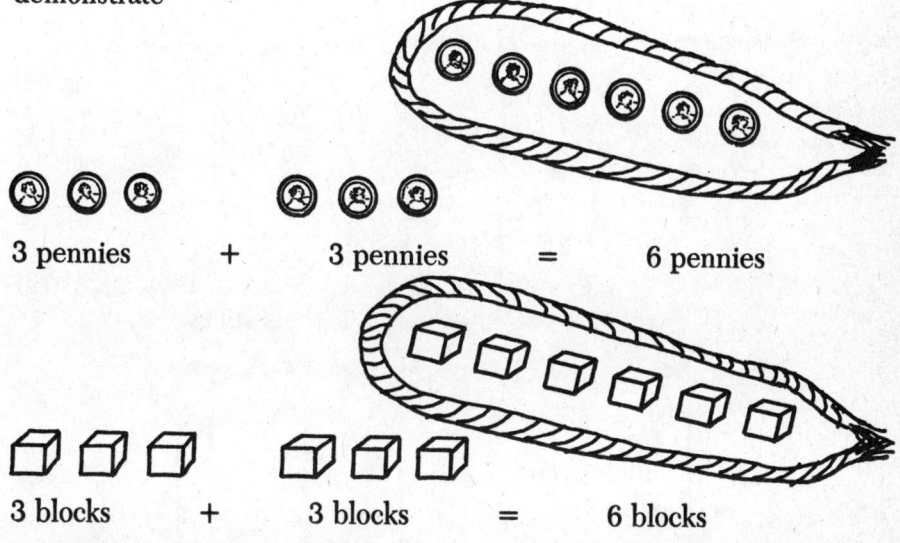

3 pennies + 3 pennies = 6 pennies

3 blocks + 3 blocks = 6 blocks

Demonstrate 3 groups of 4 beans = 12 beans. Use pictorial dittos for several days to demonstrate. Have the children make pictures cutting objects from old workbooks or contruction paper to demonstrate several facts (at least 2 per child on 5 successive days). Have child commit multiplication facts to memory.

Skill 16. Demonstrate that if you begin with 6 and divide them into 2 groups there will be 3 in each group.

$2 \times 3 = 6$
$3 \times 2 = 6$

$6 \div 2 = 3$
$6 \div 3 = 2$

Skill 17. Teach place value ones, tens, hundreds, thousands.

As the children add 3 digits to 3 digits, do a lot of verbalizing about hundreds. Some math programs do a good pictorial job of hundreds, tens, ones and it is well to consult and use them.[13]

Skill 18. Introduce children to simple word problems. If need be, read them to the child. Have him draw pictures demonstrating the process. Some examples of simple word problems follow.

1. 6 boys. 4 girls. How many kids in all? (Child draws.)

2. 9 chairs. 15 people. How many must stand? (Child draws.)

3. 6 sticks of gum. You share them with a friend. How many will each of you get? (Child draws and labels sticks.)

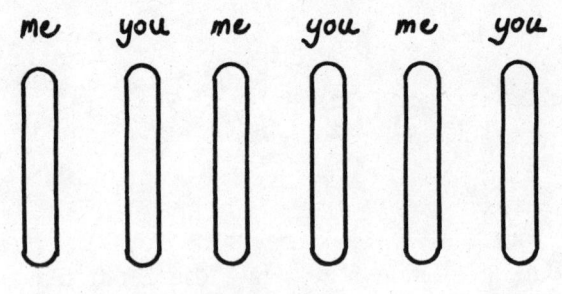

SUMMARY

1. Develop the remedial child's ability to visualize what numbers stand for.
2. Give multiple manipulative and pictorial experiences to assist in this visualization process.

---

[13]*Mathematics Around Us* (Palo Alto, Calif: Scott-Foresman, 1975).

How to Teach Remedial Arithmetic

3. Teach processes such as joining (+, ×) and separating (− and ÷) by manipulative and pictorial demonstration.
4. Teach the child to verbalize the things he is doing with numbers.

If you keep these principles in mind, you can make successive lessons meaningful to the child using a regular textbook series. For example, when you approach fractions and decimals, the use of a pie graph can help the child visualize the fact that .50 is the same amount as half (a concept the child has already met). Fractions should be taught daily for at least several weeks with the use of pictures.

Have the child see he can visually move one piece up so the final answer is 1½.

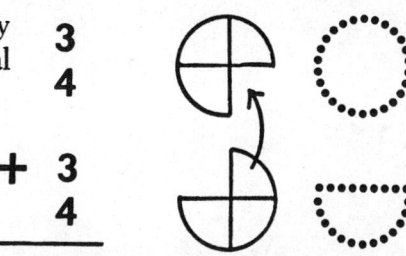

When you teach ⅔ × 15, use multiple pictorial practice like

Child colors 2 out of each 3.

$$\tfrac{2}{3} \text{ of } 15 = 10$$

When teaching long division, I suggest this method; based on your previous instruction this approach is now understandable.

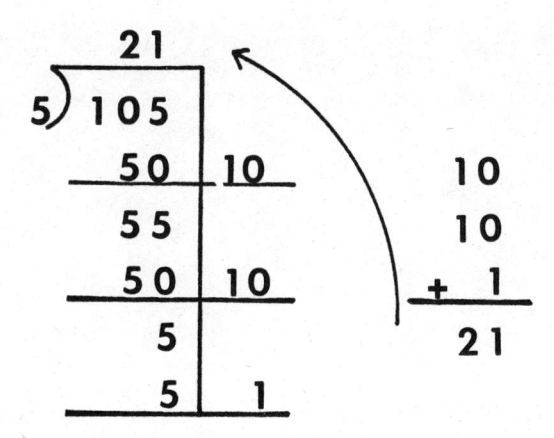

When working with the remedial child, it is far better to have him do 5 problems each day for several days—even weeks—in a row than to have him do 50 problems one day and not return to that kind of problem for several days.

It is also to be remembered that the remedial child must have a short weekly or twice-weekly drill to retain a skill he has mastered previously.

Approaching math in the manner outlined in this chapter may have an interesting serendipity effect—you too may feel more inspired to teach the subject.

The step-by-step program outlined in this chapter will provide a firm foundation for the child's future math growth. At this stage, he will be able to begin regular fourth grade math material.

12

Improving Visual Perception And Motor Control With No-Fail Art Activities

"Mike, that's really nice. How do you feel about it?" Mike looks at his tempera painting and, satisfied, says "I like it."

So often elementary school children want to destroy their art work, feeling it to be worthless and inferior. In a short time some children "turn off" on art and do not want to attempt other projects.

The purpose of this chapter is to suggest techniques for development of artistic interest. These techniques are accompanied by specific project suggestions. The projects chosen have been favorites among the children I've taught and are "no fail" experiences. They can renew a child's interest in art because he can succeed where previously he has felt inadequate.

General Considerations

Art in the elementary school should help the child become aware of his inner feelings about color, shape, textures and media. *By experimentation and self-critiquing* the child will develop an awareness of his preferences. *By careful guidance* the child will have an opportunity to develop an appreciation of the works of others.

Your role in this process is to provide children with

1. Time,
2. Space,
3. A variety of media, introduced one at a time,
4. A chance to view several art works using a given media (input),

5. Freedom to experiment within reasonable limits (output), and
6. An opportunity to discuss their product with others.

The grading of an art project is an unwise practice. The child will try to please you, and this leads to self-devaluation if you give a particular effort a low grade. Additionally, this practice limits the child's freedom of expression because he doesn't develop feelings for his likes/dislikes. It is more helpful for you to say, "I like the way you placed your objects," or "These colors blend well."

You can help the child look at his project from a different perspective, e.g., the child may need help to examine fine details in order to make his picture more natural looking. Occasionally, you must insist that a given child produce something. The child with very low self-esteem or who has had no success with art in the past needs your close supervision to overcome his inertia.

A second technique that you may use involves having the child keep an art folder where he stores all art pieces he produces. Periodically, you and the student will take time to look through that folder together. This is easy to do—perhaps you make a point to see only one child a day, but that child feels important—his work becomes a personal thing he shares with you. You may direct his development with questions such as, "How do you feel about the colors you chose?" "If we were to do this project again, how would you do it differently?" "Did you particularly like someone else's picture and why?"

It has been my experience that children give better effort and get better art results if they are required to be still and quiet and to work alone for the basic art time. There is value in following up the quiet art period with a time when the children can move about and share their results.

Tempera Painting

Projects: **Blending, Making Secondary Colors from Primary Color**

Time: 40-60 minutes per session

In the beginning, help students learn to enjoy color, lines, shapes, textures. Show examples of nonrepresentational art and explain that many people enjoy pictures that don't look realistic.

A good way to begin is to put out tempera paint. On waxed paper, give each child a small quantity of white tempera and a small quantity of a colored tempera (orange *or* brown *or* blue make good starters). By only giving the child two colors he is forced to experiment with lines, shapes, lights and darks, textures (allow him to try painting with popsicle sticks, brushes, sponges, his fingers, etc.). Vocabulary development should be kept in mind. The meaning of shade, tone, pale, bright, dull fits well within these lessons.

Often a frame cut from contrasting construction paper can highlight a student's work in a beautiful way. Additionally, when you take time to frame a student's work, the child feels important!

In Mike's case, when I looked at his tempera work it looked like a beautiful orange sunset. I showed him how to add a simple bird figure and presto! The simple background became a magical and valuable piece of art to this child. Mike also learned the meaning of contrast, foreground/background in this lesson because we talked about these words.

When showing a child how to do something like making a bird, be careful to show him on scrap paper, then have him practice on scrap paper before he attempts to put the object on his good paper.

Tempera painting should be done for several sessions in a row. For the first session, you might put out orange and white paint. For the second session, you might put out blue and white paint. By the third session, you might want to put out blue, yellow, and white. You are now ready to help the child learn about blending blue and yellow into green. Again, a magical world appears before his eyes. In a later session, he'll discover what happens when red and yellow come together. Thus, you begin with the concept of primary colors red/blue/yellow and move the child via self-discovery to secondary colors green/purple/orange. A last stage may be to show the child that brown can be obtained by "messing around" with red/blue/yellow until you have the proper combination of the three colors. In this "messing around," much is learned about shades.

Help the child experiment also with diluting colors with varying amounts of water to obtain differing shades.

Projects: **Fingerpainting with Tempera/Vano Starch 1/2:1/2**
Time: 60 minutes

Using only 1 color demonstrate designs in fingerpaint such as wind-blowing, fire-burning, rain-falling. Vary colors to create a mood—wind-blowing might be in greens, fire-burning might be in oranges or reds, rain-falling might be in blue or gray.

Try fist, palms, fingertips. The feels and smells of the project make a good language development lesson as well. Develop concept of mood particularly with gray vs. blue rain.

Project: **String Art (Abstract)**
Time: 25 minutes

Paint a piece of string 2 or 3 feet long with powdered tempera. Place it on a piece of paper; fold the paper over the string. Be sure that one end of the string extends beyond the bottom of the paper. Press down firmly on the top sheet of paper and pull the string out. *Variation:* Have child use more than one string, more than one color.

Develop concept of abstract (however it turns out) vs. representational art (must look like something).

Mosaics

Project: **Design with Construction Paper**
Time: 60 minutes

Mosaic work requires some pre-preparation by the teacher. First, obtain several boxes so that you can cut and store mosaic pieces. I have found a shoe box containing all colors can be shared by 4 children. Next, pre-cut pieces of colored construction paper. (I cut strips ½ inch wide—can be cut on paper cutter—then I let my "helpers" cut these strips into squares ½" by ½".)

From the library or elsewhere, obtain a few samples of mosaics. A fish or a flower are easy designs.

By allowing the children time to look at each others' work at the end of each session, children get ideas they'd like to try. Mosaic art should be pursued for a minimum of two sessions.

Project: **Owl (Seeds)**
Time: 60 minutes 2 days in a row

Prepare an owl ditto. Have child reverse ditto, color back lightly

No-Fail Art Activities   **199**

with black crayon being careful to color lightly but directly behind lines you drew. By placing the ditto on a large sheet the child can trace over your lines transferring design to bristol board or heavy paper (which will support the weight of sunflower seeds).

Child applies, with glue, bottle caps for eyes, pet store sunflower seeds (overlapping with points down so *texture* is like feathers of owl), orange construction paper nose. After entire body of owl is finished child can add a small diameter stick and overlap stick with orange feet so owl appears to perch.

Language development lesson regarding words *reverse, overlap, perch, texture* can accompany project.

Tissue Paper

Project: **Trees**
Time: 60 minutes
Prior to doing this project go out and look at some trees.

Cut the trunk and branches of the trees from construction paper. Glue trunks on paper. *Cover the* whole paper with starch and then tear pieces of colored tissue paper to suggest leaves. Place pieces to vary shades. Use yellow green color to suggest sun on the leaves and dark green colors to suggest the shadowy parts.

Project: **Tissue Paper Flowers**
Time: 25 minutes

This project initially should be pre-prepared. (At a later date students can repeat it without teacher preparation.) Take colored tissue paper, at lease 12 thicknesses. Cut in squares 4" by 4" and put a staple in the center to hold all thickness.

Show the students how to cut a circle. Cut all layers into circles with sharp scissors. Then, they pick up the top thickness and crumple it upward. The second layer is crumpled upward. Continue till all layers have been crumpled. In future session the children will enjoy varying colors and sizes of flowers, then making three-dimensional pictures with them by applying them to a background, adding leaves/stems. These make nice cards for special occasions.

Stitchery

Project: **Sock Puppets/Geometric Stitchery Designs**
Time: 40 minutes

Many art projects can be developed from stitchery. The initial steps, however, involve teaching children to thread a needle, tie a bow, sew on a button; sew two straight edges of fabric together, make tiny even stitches.

After the above skills are taught, children enjoy making sock puppets or pictures using colorful thread.

Styrofoam

Project: **Free Form Sculpture**
Time: 40 minutes

Obtain a box of styrofoam packing pieces; the school library or district materials supply will save this for you if you request it. You also need bases (styrofoam cups do nicely). Buy colored toothpicks and distribute an average of 20 per child.

Make it clear the sculpture they make does not have to look like something—it is just a fun design

Project: **Snowman**
Time: 40 minutes

Children use glue to put bits of styrofoam in place on paper to form a snowman. A nose of orange construction paper can be added.

No-Fail Art Activities

Black construction paper eyes, hat and buttons. Sticks for hands. Paints can add a background.

Construction Paper

Project: **Positive-Negative Art**
Time: 30 minutes

Make several examples of positive-negative art ahead. Precut some black strips of construction paper 4" × 11½" to be pasted on white paper 8" × 11½".

Demonstrate on black sheet the cutting of a design any way you feel like doing. Keep the piece that fell out. Reverse it. Paste both on white paper.

Display all results. Children are very innovative. Much vocabulary development can occur in such terms as half/whole/reverse.

Project: **Paper Weaving**
Time: 40 minutes

Give each child 2 pieces of contrasting construction paper: one piece cut into 1" wide strips lengthwise, the other piece slit at 1" intervals widthwise. Alternating in and out, child weaves a pattern.

Project: 3-Dimensional Flowers
Time: 2 sessions, 40 minutes each
Demonstrate 3 kinds of flowers.

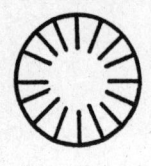

Roll into circle.

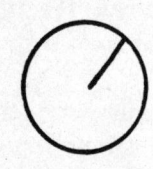

Cut and roll.

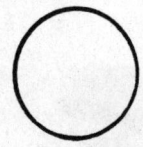

Fold in half.

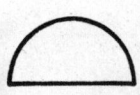

Fold half this way and cut.   Yields

Project: Lines and Shapes
Time: 30-40 minutes

Talk about contrasting colors, lines (thick vs. narrow), straight, curvy, horizontal, vertical, diagonal, shapes. Using some pre-prepared samples such as these, discuss lines and shapes used. Remove samples so children will use their imagination; allow children to create their own designs. They can cut, paste, draw or follow any other creative idea they may come up with.

No-Fail Art Activities

As feedback ask children to show you a horizontal line or curvy line (describe some line they used).

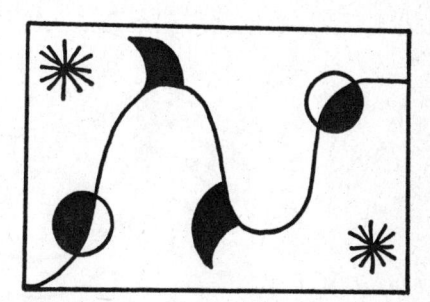

Project: **Hanging Plaques**
Time: 30 minutes

Fold a piece of black and a piece of colored construction paper in half. (Put one inside the other.) Cut many holes of varying sizes into the folded edge. Place another piece or pieces of colored paper in between these cut-out designs. Fasten to string.

Language development: mobile (moves), companion words auto*mobile*.

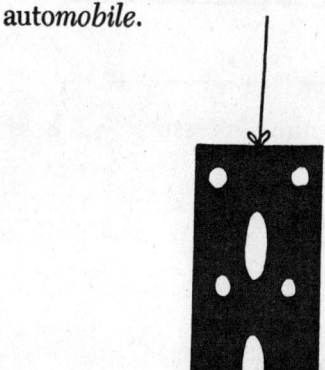

Project: **Birds**
Time: 30 minutes

Place one 18 × 12 sheet each of purple, blue, green, yellow, orange, pink paper together. Cut in strips lengthwise (¾" wide). Put one staple in about 2 inches from an end to hold strips together.

By pushing some strips upward, some down child gets a bird. Curl tail feathers by stripping them with scissors. Young children need help curling paper.

staple

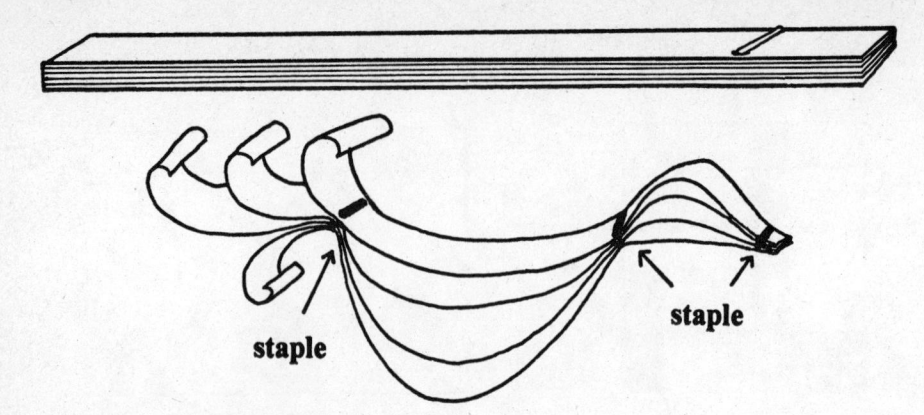

staple

Project: **Pressure Design**
Time: 40 minutes

Cut strips of contruction paper (multiple colors) about 1″ wide. Show children how to lock them by making a cut in each end, folding ends together and inserting slots (make sure tabs are on inside so circles made are round.

Other strips are folded loosely. Fit together; "pressure" will hold them.

Project: **Creativity with Paper**
Time: 40 minutes

Demonstrate that construction paper can be cut, torn and curled by stripping it between scissor blade and thumb. Then ask children to "create" using imagination to make a paper design.

Drawing

Project: **Vegetables/Fruits**
Time: 30 minutes

Teach "contour"—"Every object has a shape, an outside boundary." Keep looking at the object and draw only its shape. Add "details" later.

Repeat lesson combining more than one shape. Show how a heavy black line can be used to "emphasize" or reinforce design. Using only black, gray and white pencil marks color fruit or vegetables.

Variation: Mixed Media. Coat a paper with starch; overlap small rectangles of tissue paper and smooth them out with a brush—color will bleed if brush moves from one color tissue to another so a clean brush should be used for each color.

Cut fruit or vegetables from black construction paper. Glue them to the tissue paper background.

Project: **Perspective" Picture**
Time: 40 minutes

Demonstrate you can make a picture appear to have distance by placement of objects and use of color.

Dark colors should be placed in lower section; lighter colors higher on paper. Things far away are drawn higher and smaller.

Spirit Felt Tip Pens and Aluminum Foil

Project: **Wall Plaques/Pictures**

Begin with a design—a "no fail" experience. Teacher prepares project by stretching aluminum foil over cardboard and fastening in back with masking tape. Child makes a squiggly design on foil. If the child is reluctant, the teacher can put a black felt tip marker in the child's hand and guide the hand to make the design. Then the child uses other colors of felt markers to add color to the design.

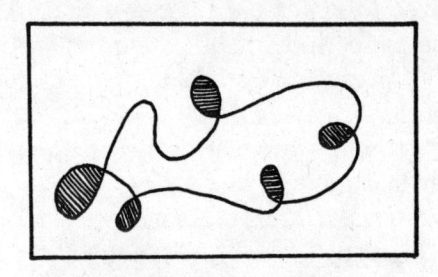

Colored Chalk

Project: **Mountain Picture Using Jagged Lines**
Time: 30-40 minutes

Give one child purple, blue and green chalk while asking another child to work with yellow, orange, red.

Talk about *mood* created by different color combination. Is one picture *exciting* while the other feels more *calm*? Language development of terms should follow.

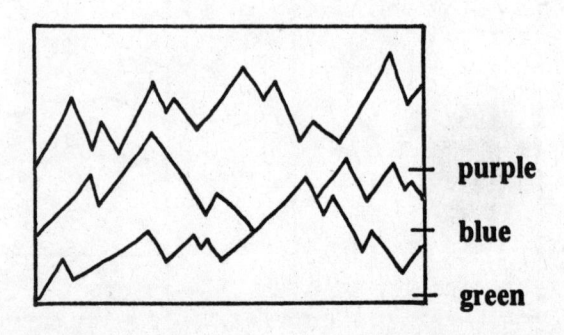

Paper Plates

Project: **Masks**
Time: 40 minutes

Decorate a paper plate, add features. Develop vocabulary with new word "features."

By cutting a wedge from the plate and taping edges you can make pointed faces.

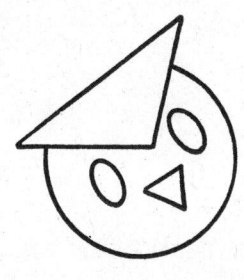

Collage

Project: **Picture with Silhouette**
Time: This project can begin as part of a planned art period and then children can work on it as they are able till it is finished.

Have children collect pieces of colored magazine advertisements. Large pieces should be reduced to smaller ones by tearing.

This size is about as large as pieces should get.

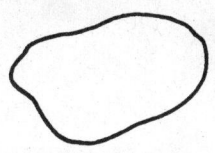

Help children become aware of *tint* or *tones* (shades).

Arrange shades of one color over an entire piece of paper, using starch or glue to hold them together (overlap edges). When background is complete, cut a figure to add to the picture. A horse, fish or bright contrasting figure looks great.

Rock Art

Project: **Paper-weight Turtles**
Time: 40-60 minutes

Find a creek bed with flat, oval shaped rocks about 2 inches long. Cut green felt bases. Glue to bottom of rock. Paint top of rock in squares with green tempera paint.

Mobiles

Project: **Fish/Bugs**

Old nylon stockings and wire join to make a mobile. Cover form with stocking pulled tight.

With construction paper and glue, add fins, tails, eyes, of bright colors. Group and hang.

Variation: Pipe cleaners, construction paper can be body of bug. Wings are made by folding heavy waxed paper in half—melting crayon inside fold for color (iron). Cut and paste wings on bug.

Braiding

Project: **Decoration for Hanging**
Time: 2 sessions, 60 minutes each

This project requires some pre-preparation or must be done by older elementary students.

Each child will need 30 strands of yarn 48" long (10 strands × 3 colors) and a ring for hanging. In addition you need 3 pinked fabric circles per child (5" diameter) 3 cotton balls and some perfume.

Run all 30 strands through ring so yarn is doubled. Braid by color. Perfume cotton balls; tie them inside circles; attach to braid at intervals. End will be a tassel.

Bread Dough

Project: **Plaque**
Time: 2 sessions, 60 minutes each

At or near time of use mix bread dough: 1 cup flour, 1 cup salt, ½ cup water. This recipe must be multiplied based on number of children. The basic recipe will serve about 5 children.

Each child forms a shape—fish, mushroom or flowers. The product is then put on a cookie sheet, coated with egg white and baked until hard. They then may be glued to a plaque (wood, heavy cardboard). Add a few dry flowers and presto! a hanging.

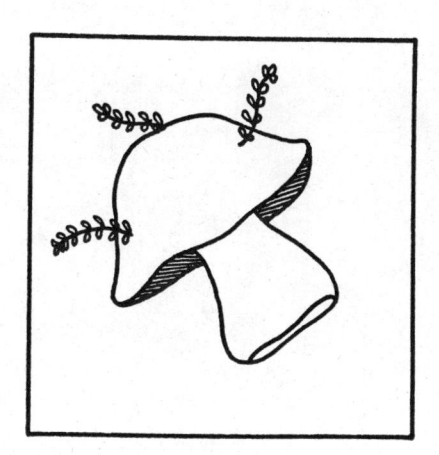

Crayon

Project: **Geometric Design**
Time: 30 minutes

Discuss "geometric" designs. Ask child to repeat design at regular "intervals." "Highlight" design with other colors.

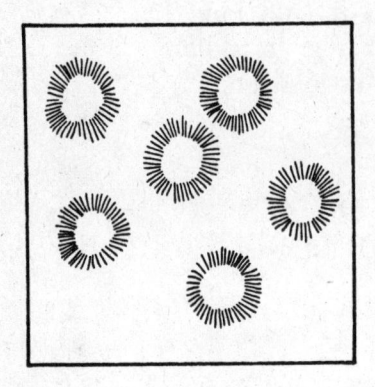

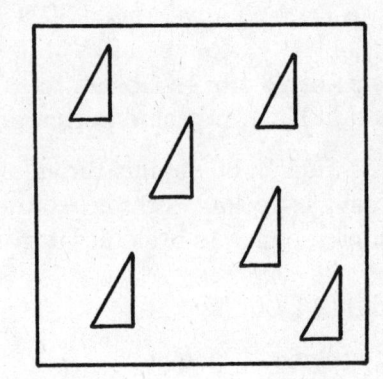

Paper and Crayon

Project: **Window Hangings**
Time: 40 minutes

Grate crayon prior to class. Get iron and heavy wax paper. Tissue paper for inside design (circles).

Place sheet of *heavy* wax paper flat. Arrange design with tissue circle and crayon gratings. Cover with second sheet of wax paper on top. Iron panel between newspapers. Add border at top and bottom to hold ends together. Hang.

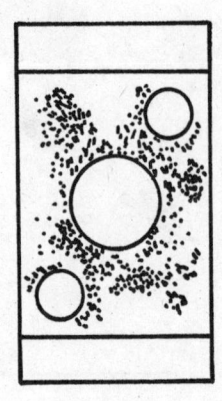

Crayon and Waterpaint

Project: **Flower/Fish/Birds**
Time: 40 minutes

Have children make a picture—large bold flowers, a fish, a bird. Press hard on bright colored crayon to color object. Using water paint wash over design with a pale coat of paint; allow bright color to come through.

* * *

Art period provides the opportunity for teacher and child to exchange ideas. Much can be done toward developing a child's visual sense and motor skills as you guide him through use of color, shape and form to make a design. The art period also provides the opportunity for language development.

Parents and children both respond positively to seeing the children's art work displayed. I stage an art show once each year—each child has one work displayed. As we review the folders each child decides which of his art pieces he wants displayed. Most children feel good about what they produced.

A Few Words in Closing

The saying, "Today is the first day of the rest of your life," could not be truer. Armed with some new ideas and techniques, you should feel more comfortable working with the child who has educational difficulties. As you see the child begin to make progress, you'll experience a deep sense of gratification. Then there comes one magical day when that child suddenly realizes he is able to be successful in areas where, heretofore, he has failed. You will know when that day has come. The child's face glows with a look so beautiful words are inadequate to describe it.

Best wishes.

Glossary of Terms

Agnosia, the inability to process information through one of the senses, even though the receiving organ does not seem to be impaired. For example, the child who must use lip-reading techniques to discriminate a "m" from a "n" because he cannot distinguish the difference although an audio-metric examination shows a normal hearing pattern.

Alexia, a total inability to read due to some cerebral damage. It may be an inability of a child to learn to read or it may occur suddenly in adults as in the case of trauma or a stroke.

Anomia, the inability to recall names of objects or words.

Aphasia, the inability to acquire/understand oral language. This may range from a total non-use of oral language to the person being able to understand what is said to him but he can not use language himself. The condition occurs due to damage in the brain's speech areas.

Apraxia, a disturbance in motor movements which is reflected in poor gross or fine motor control.

Closure, the ability to fill in gaps. For example, to look at a part of a thing and recognize it as the whole (such as half a tree), or to fill in a blank in a sentence with the correct word.

Constancy, the inability to recognize the sameness of shapes/sounds if they appear in another context from the one in which they were learned.

Dyscalculia, the inability to perform math operations. A sample symptom is transposing order of numbers, 36 is 63.

Dysgraphia, the inability to control fine movements of the hand so pencil/paper work is of extremely poor quality.

Dyslexia, similar to alexia, but different in degree. Dyslexia is an extremely slow acquisition of reading skills, but alexia is a total inability to read.

Electroencephalogram, (EEG) a medical procedure (nonpainful) whereby neurological brain damage may be discovered.

Figure-Ground distraction, the subject is unable to focus his attention on a task due to distracting influences (visual or auditory) in the environment. For example, many children require a marker when reading to blot out the distraction created by other words on the page.

Impulsivity, acting on impulse, with no prior consideration of possible untoward consequences.

Laterality, the inability to distinguish left from right sides of the body. This confusion can be overcome with skillful teaching directed at developing an awareness.

Modalities, the channels through which we perceive—visual, auditory, tactile (touch).

Perception, taking in information through our senses and processing that information in such a way that it has meaning to us.

Perseveration, the continuation of an activity beyond the saturation point; an inability to stop an activity.

Phonetics, the study of the sounds of letters and groups of letters.

Spatial disorder, an inability to conceptualize oneself as the body relates to other objects, time, place.

Index

A

Absences, frequent, 14, 15
Abstract thinking, 144
Academic assessment, 21-22
Accountability, 35
Achievement tests, 21
Activity level, 20
Adjustment problems, 147-148
Aggression, 147
Aluminum foil, 206
Anemia, 145
Anxiety, signs, 15
Arithmetic:
    add numbers 1-100, 188-189
    add sums less than 10, 186
    carrying, 189
    count from, 1-100, 188
    counting by 10's to 100, 189
    counting games, 184
    dime stands for 10, 189
    dividing 6 into 2 groups, 191-192
    foot ruler and yard ruler, 190-191
    going *too* fast, 184
    guesstimating, 185
    half, 187-188
    insufficient drill, 184
    joining or separating, 185
    manipulative experiences, 184
    more/less concept, 184
    numbers 1-10, 185-186
    place value, 189, 192
    real coins, 190
    relate multiplication to adding, 191
    sequential activities, 185-192
    simple word problems, 192
    subtract amounts less than 10, 186-187
    subtracting with borrowing, 190
    subtracting without borrowing, 190
    sums less than 99, 189
    TV programs, 184
    visualize what numbers stand for, 184
Arm muscles, 112

Art activities:
    aluminum foil, 206
    braiding, 209
    bread dough, 209
    collage, 207
    colored chalk, 206
    construction paper, 201-204
    drawing, 205
    mobiles, 208
    mosaics, 198-199
    paper plates, 207
    rock art, 207-208
    spirit felt tip pens, 206
    stitchery, 200
    styrofoam, 200-201
    tempera painting, 196-198
    tissue paper, 199-200
    your role, 195-196
Assessment:
    academic, 21-22
    intellectual capacity, 22
    preferred learning style, 22-28
Assignments, unfinished, 15
Association:
    auditory, 101-105
    visual, 85-88
Attention problems:
    emotional adjustment, 147-148
    epilepsy, 144, 145-146
    hyperactivity, 143, 144-145
    hypoactivity, 143, 145
    perseveration, 146-147
Audiologist, 90
Auditory perception:
    association, 101-105
    audiologist, 90
    beginning sounds of words, 96
    child's speech, 90
    closure, 101-105
    definition, 89
    direction from which sound comes, 91
    directions on board, 91

Auditory perception (*cont.*)
  discrimination problems, 91-96
  distractibility, 96-98
  figure-ground, 96-98
  get child's attention, 91
  inappropriate answers, 89
  individual sounds, 93
  learning to listen, 90
  lectures and stories, 89
  less permanent information, 90
  letter-sound discrimination, 92-93
  like and different sounds, 89, 91, 95
  long time in answering, 89
  math presented orally, 89
  memory, 98-101
  "mis" in words, 94
  n/m, b/p, v/f, 91
  nonsense rhymes, 92
  notes kept by child, 91
  oral directions, 89
  phonetics, 89
  questions asked orally, 89
  rhyming activities, 94, 95
  short vowel sounds, 89, 91, 93
  sources of sounds, 91
  syllables, 93
  visual stimuli, 90, 91
  where word ends, 90
  word endings, 96
  word lists, 93
Aversive techniques, 39-40, 147

B

B, D confusion, 72-73
Balance beam, 109
Balls, motor control, 111
Baseball, 112
Bean bags, motor control, 111
Behavior problems, 143-148
  (*see also* Attention problems)
Body awareness:
  cutting experiences, 115
  "Do as I Do" game, 113
  dot-to-dot activities, 115
  drawing, 113-114
  identifying body parts, 113
  identifying objects by feel, 117
  importance, 63

Body awareness (*cont.*)
  jacks and darts, 115
  Japanese paperfolding, 115
  lessons on body's systems, 113
  manipulating body through space, 114
  reproducing patterns, 114-115
  right and left concept, 115-116
Braiding, 209
Brain, lesion, 144

C

Carelessness, motor skills, 122
Causation, 19
Children, screening, 15-17
Classroom management:
  corrections and review, 32
  discipline, 38-43
    (*see also* Discipline)
  feedback, 34, 38, 39
  honesty, 31
  lesson plan, 33-35
  parent volunteers, 36-38
  promises, 31
  record-keeping, 35-36
  sharing personal experiences, 32
  structure, 30
  student tutors, 36-38
  teacher-pupil relationship, 30-33
  verbal commendation, 32
  warmth, 32-33
Class study, preliminary, 13
Closure:
  auditory, 101-105
  visual, 85-88
Collage, 207
Coloring, 120
Commendation, verbal, 32
Competencies, 44-59
  (*see also* Skills development)
Competition, 112
Conceptual thinking, 124-142
  (*see also* Language development)
Constancy, visual, 80-82
Construction paper, 201-204
Copying from board, 71
Corrections, 32
Counseling, 147

Index

Cruelty, 147
Crying daily, 15
Cursive writing, 119
Cutting experiences, 115

D

Darts, 115
Defecating, 15
Destructiveness, 147
Developmental lag, 19
Diagnosis:
  academic assessment, 21-22
  activity level, 20
  cannot name common objects, 15
  causation, 19
  crying daily, 15
  environmental upsets, 14
  fine motor control, 20
  frequent absences, 14, 15
  frequent tardiness, 15
  goal, 19
  gross motor control, 20
  incontinence, 15
  individual educational plan, 28-29
  intellectual capacity, 22
  Key Math Diagnostic Test, 21
  misbehaving habitually, 15
  motivational problems, 14
  Peabody Individual Achievement Test, 21
  physical examination, 20-21
  preferred learning style, 22-28
  preliminary class study, 13-15
  problem areas, 13
  repeated failure, 14
  screening children, 15-17
  significantly inferior work, 15
  signs of extreme anxiety, 15
  unfinished assignments, 15
  Wide-Range Achievement Test, 21
  WISC, 22
  Woodcock Reading Test, 21
  working with parents, 17-20
Diagnostic/prescriptive teaching, 33
Diet, 145
Directions, auditory perception, 89, 91
Discipline:
  accepting responsibility, 42

Discipline (cont.)
  afternoon activities, 39
  anecdotal records, 42
  aversive techniques, 39-40
  be human being, 42
  careful lesson planning, 38
  cooperative feeling, 42
  detentions, 39
  don't use class time, 41
  feelings of self-esteem, 38
  handle it yourself, 41
  ignoring, 39, 40
  length of instructional periods, 38
  modeling, 40, 41
  morning hours, 39
  negative feedback, 39
  not in front of classmates, 41
  principles, 40-43
  reprimand, 39
  rewards, 39
  same day, 41
  social disapproval, 40
  tattling, 41-42
  time-out, 39, 40
Discrimination:
  auditory, 91-96
  visual, 69-72
Distractibility, 96-98
Disturbed children, 147-148
Dittoes, 120, 123
"Do as I Do" game, 113
Dodgeball, 112
Dot-to-dot activities, 115, 122
Double vision, 71
Drawing, 113-114, 205

E

Educational plan, individual, 28-29
Emotional adjustment, 147-148
Empathy, 64
Encephalographic examination, 144
Environmental upsets, 14
Epilepsy, 144, 145-146
Evaluation by teacher, 65-66

F

Failure, 14, 64-65
Family Service Assn. of America, 147

Index

Feedback, 34, 38, 39, 63, 65
Feingold, Benjamin, 145
Figure-ground problems:
   auditory, 96-98
   visual, 76-80
Fine motor skills, 20, 117-123
   (*see also* Motor controls)
Finishing assignments, 15
Forms, 35
Frisbee, 112
Frostig, Marianne, 77

G

Grand mal, 145
Gross motor skills, 20, 107-112
   (*see also* Motor controls)
Guidance, 147

H

Handwriting:
   carelessness, 122
   causes of difficulty, 118
   cursive, 119
   fine motor control, 117
   left-handed child, 119-120
   manuscript, 119
   perception of letters and words, 122-123
   poor motor skills, 120-122
   spatial perception, 123
   testing, 118-119
   visual memory, 122-123
Heredity, 19
Honesty, 31
Hoola Hoop, 112
Hopping, 112
Hyperactive child, 143, 144-145
Hypoactive child, 143, 145

I

Impulsivity, 147
Incontinence, 15
Individual educational plan, 28-29
Individualizing instruction, 66
Instruction, individualizing, 66
Intellectual capacity, 22
Inversions, visual, 70, 74

J

Jacks, 115
Jumping, 112
Jump ropes, 111
Juvenile Probation Department, 147

K

Key Math Diagnostic Test, 21
Kickball, 112

L

Ladder, motor control, 110-111
Language
   (*see* Reading/Writing/Language)
Language development:
   activities, 127-141
      animals of prey, 137
      bird feathers, 128
      butterflies, 140
      cereal box designs, 128
      cloud patterns, 131
      colors of leaf, 130
      comparing apples, 132
      container size and shape, 129
      continuous lines, 130
      contours, 138
      curved surface, 135, 137
      demonstrate tones, 136
      discuss shapes, 128, 131
      discuss veins, 140
      drawing stick pictures, 136
      fabric scraps, 128
      favorite colors, 128-129
      favorite pictures, 133
      feeling items, 129, 131, 132
      finger painting, 138
      fingerprints, 138-139
      fish pictures, 133
      foliage patterns, 130
      foods, 134, 137
      fruit-prints, 130
      garage tools, 134
      group drawing, 138
      guessing color by smell, 133
      hard/soft, 131
      homemade guitar, 134
      identify cool, warm and cold, 139

Index

Language development *(cont.)*
    identify sounds, 129, 134-135, 139
    imaginary creatures, 132
    Indian masks, 135
    Indian names, 135
    jewelery, 131
    kitchen tools, 134
    like and different flowers, 140
    like and different nuts, 132
    like and different plants, 131
    listening to music, 138
    looking at trees, 131
    looking for good pictures, 129-130
    meanings of word, 140-141
    modeling clay, 136
    molds/frames/forms, 140
    movie sound track, 132
    opaque/translucent, 136-137
    opposites, 139
    ornaments, 137
    overlapping, 135
    painting on wet paper, 133
    paste shapes into design, 128
    pipe cleaner designs, 128
    playing water-filled glasses, 134
    scariest sound, 132
    sea shells, 133
    seasons and clothing, 130
    skeletons, 134
    soap bubbles, 133
    sports pictures, 135
    sprouting or growing, 139
    Statues game, 135
    stencils, 131
    straight surface, 135
    textures, 131
    3 sizes of boxes, 133
    tracing hand, 132
    unshelled peanuts, 128
    value, 136
    vegetable prints, 127
    yarn designs, 127
  class discussion, 125-127
  recognizing problems, 124-125
Learning style, preferred, 22-28
Lectures, auditory perception, 89
Left and right concept, 115-116
Left-handed child, 119-120
Lesion, brain, 144
Lesson plan, 33-35
Letter confusion, 70, 74-75
Letters, faulty perception, 122
Letter-sound discrimination, 92-93
Loner, 147
Lying, 147

M

Malnourishment, 145
Management of classroom, 30-43
  (*see also* Classroom management)
Manuscript writing, 119
Mat activities, 112
Math, auditory perception, 89
Mathematics skills:
  arithmetic, remedial, 184-194
  (*see also* Arithmetic)
  Grade 1, 46, 47
  Grade 2, 51
  Grade 3, 53
  Grade 4, 55-56
  Grade 5, 57-58
  Grade 6, 58-59
Math test, 21
Memory:
  auditory, 98-101
  visual, 83, 85, 122-123
Misbehaving habitually, 15
Mobiles, 208
Mosaics, 198-199
Motivational problems, 14
Motor controls:
  art activities, 195-211
    (*see also* Art activities)
  fine, 117-123
    careless child, 122
    coloring, 120
    faulty perception of letters and words, 122-123
    handwriting, 117-123
    (*see also* Handwriting)
    spatial perception problems, 123
    stencils and dittoes, 120
    visual memory problems, 122-123
  gross, 107-112
    additional activities, 112
    arm muscles, 112

Motor controled (*cont.*)
  gross (*cont.*)
    balance beam, 108, 109
    balls or bean bags, 108, 111
    equipment, 108
    Hoola Hoop, 108, 112
    jump ropes, 108, 111
    ladder, 108, 110-111
    mat activities, 112
    mats or carpeted area, 108
    old tires, 108, 109-110
    push-ups, 112
    scooter board, 108, 112
  importance, 63
  in-school evaluation, 20
  mid-first grade skills, 107

N

Naming objects, 15
Neurological impress:
  copying machine, 177
  drill, 179
  first day, 177-178
  give clues, 179
  help child build units, 179
  multiple exposures to word, 178-179
  older students, 177
  reading grade level of 2.0 or up, 177
  record-keeping system, 177
  remedial reading, 177-183
  reward system, 177
  sample paragraphs, 179-183
  second day and subsequent days, 178
  set of cards for each child, 177
  syllabication rules, 179
Neurologist, 144
Nonsense rhymes, 92
Notes kept by child, 91
Nutritional factors, 19

O

Origami, 115

P

P, Q, 73
Paperfolding, 115
Parents, working with, 17-20
Parent volunteers, 36-38

Patterns, reproducing, 114-115
Peabody Individual Achievement Test, 21
Pediatric neurologist, 144
Perception, 127-141
Perseveration, 146-147
Petit mal, 145
Phonetics, 89
Physical examination, 20-21
Plan, individual educational, 28-29
Probation officers, 147
Problem areas, 13
Promises, 31
Psychomotor seizure, 146
Psychomotor skills:
  Grade 1, 45, 47
  Grade 2, 50-51
  Grade 3, 52
  Grade 4, 55
  Grade 5, 57
  Grade 6, 58
Punctuation disregarded, 71, 76
Punishment, immediate, 41, 147
Push-ups, 112

R

Reading:
  accuracy, 176
  activities, 155-176
  advantages of program, 151
  all child's modalities, 151
  assume nothing, 179
  clues, 179
  consonant and vowel sounds, 152-155
  drill, 179
  feedback, 177
  general principles for teaching, 176-177
  give help, 176
  go slow, 176
  help child build units, 179
  markers, 176
  multiple exposures to word, 178-179
  neurological impress, 177-183
  peer-relations within group, 177
  permanent bulletin board, 151
  program-in fun, 177

Index

Reading (*cont.*)
  reinforcement, 176
  results in short time, 151
  short vowel cards, 151
  syllabication rules, 179
  test, 21
  3-4 elements in day, 176
  two 25 minute daily sessions, 176
  visual supports, 151
  week's spelling, 177
  work for mastery, 176
Reading/Writing/Language:
  Grade 1, 44
  Grade 2, 49-51
  Grade 3, 51-54
  Grade 4, 54-56
  Grade 5, 56-58
  Grade 6, 58
Record-keeping, 35-36
Referral, physical examination, 20-21
Relay races, 112
Remediation
  (*see* Reading; Arithmetic)
Reversals, visual, 70
Review, 32
Reward, 39, 147
Rhymes, nonsense, 92
Rhyming activities, 94, 96
Right and left concept, 115-116
Ritalin, 144-145
Rock art, 207-208

S

Scooter board, 112
Screening children, 15-17
Seizures, epileptic, 144
Sequencing problem, 70, 75-76
Short vowel sounds, 89, 91, 93
Skills development:
  Grade 1, 44-49
  Grade 2, 49-51
  Grade 3, 51-54
  Grade 4, 54-56
  Grade 5, 56-58
  Grade 6, 58-59
Skipping, 112
Soccer, 112
Somersaults, 112

Sound
  (*see* Auditory perception)
Spatial perception, 123
Spelling:
  Grade 1, 46, 47-48
  Grade 2, 51
  Grade 3, 54
  Grade 4, 56
  Grade 5, 58
  Grade 6, 59
Stealing, 147
Stencils, 120
Stitchery, 200
Stories, auditory perception, 89
Structure, child's need, 30-31
Student tutors, 36-38
Styrofoam, 200-201
Syllables, 93

T

Tardiness, 15
Task-analytic teaching, 33
Teacher-pupil relationship, 30-33
Tempera painting, 196-198
Therapy, child in, 147
Time out, 39, 40, 148
Tires, motor skills, 109-110
Tissue paper, 199-200
Trauma, 19
Tutors, student, 36-38

U

Urinating, 15

V

Visual perception:
  art activities, 195-211
  (*see also* Art activities)
  association, 85-88
  B, D confusion, 72-73
  blurry print, 71
  closing one eye, 71
  closure, 85-88
  constancy, 80-82
  definition, 68
  figure-ground deficits, 76-80
  frequently losing place, 71
  Frostig, 77

Visual perception (*cont.*)
  headaches, 71
  hitting or catching ball, 71
  inability to copy from board, 71
  inversions, 70, 74
  letter confusion, 70, 74-75
  memory, 83, 85, 122-123
  opthalmologist, 71
  P, Q, 73
  punctuation disregarded, 71, 76
  recognition of deficits, 69-72
  red, itchy eyes, 71
  resting head on one arm, 71
  reversals, 70
  seeing double, 71
  sequencing problem, 70, 75-76
  squinting or blinking, 71
  symptoms, 70-71
  teacher-made test, 69
  tiredness when reading, 71
  turning head to one side, 71
  when reading aloud, 70-71

Visual stimuli, 90, 91
Vitamin therapy, 145
Volunteers, parent, 36-38

W

Warmth, 32-33
Wechsler Intelligence Scale for Children, 22
Wheelbarrow, 112
Why Your Child Is Hyperactive, 145
Wide-Range Achievement Test, 21
Withdrawal, 15, 147
Woodcock Reading Test, 21
Words:
  endings, 96
  faulty perception, 122-123
  lists, 93
Writing
  (*see* Reading/Writing/Language; Handwriting)